scjc

ENTERTAINMENT ENCYCLOPEDIAS

THE ACTOR ENCYCLOPEDIA

BY DONNA B. McKINNEY

Encyclopedias

An Imprint of Abdo Reference
abdobooks.com

TABLE OF CONTENTS

ACTORS AND HOLLYWOOD

Acting is when a person plays a character for an audience's enjoyment. This practice has been around since ancient times. For centuries, actors have used their movements and voices to bring characters to life. Today, actors perform in plays on stages, in movies shown at theaters, and on television programs streamed into countless homes.

The first movies were in black and white. They often did not have dialogue that could be heard. Developments in technology continue to change film.

Hollywood is a part of Los Angeles, California. People have been making movies there since the early 1900s. Today, major movie studios operate from Hollywood, including Universal Studios and Warner Bros. Studios.

Numerous people are needed to make movies and television shows. They include directors, writers, producers, set designers, camera operators, costume designers, makeup artists, and editors. While all these jobs are important, it's the actors who get most of the spotlight. Over their careers, actors may play various roles. They may appear in many movies, plays, or television shows. They captivate audiences worldwide and become household names.

People use high-tech equipment to shoot movies.

JULIE ANDREWS

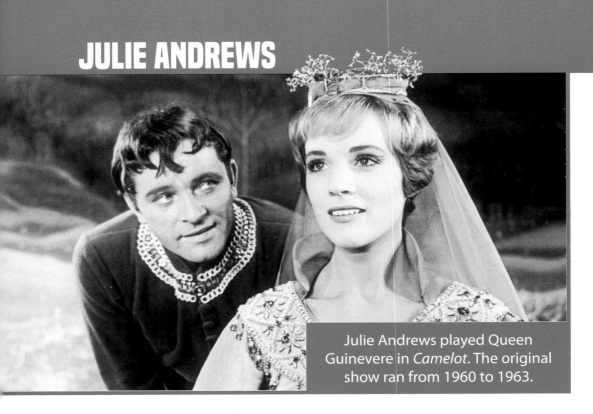

Julie Andrews played Queen Guinevere in *Camelot*. The original show ran from 1960 to 1963.

Julie Andrews's career in movies and on the stage has spanned seven decades. She is known for both her acting and singing talents. As a young adult, she began performing on Broadway and was praised for her stage performances in *My Fair Lady* and *Camelot*. Andrews starred in her first movie, *Mary Poppins*, in 1964. The next year she appeared in the classic film *The Sound of Music*. Andrews sang in both movies.

DID YOU KNOW?

The Academy Awards, also called the Oscars, is an award ceremony that takes place every year. There are more than 20 award categories, including Best Actor and Best Actress. People consider an Oscar to be the most prestigious award someone in the film industry can win.

WIDE-RANGING TALENTS

Andrews's wide-ranging talents include acting, singing, voice acting, and even writing books. In 2022, the American Film Institute honored Andrews with a Lifetime Achievement Award. This award is given to people who have made exceptional contributions to the film industry.

Andrews was nominated for an Academy Award for her performance in *The Sound of Music*.

AT A GLANCE

Notable Films: *Mary Poppins* (1964), *The Americanization of Emily* (1964), *The Sound of Music* (1965), *Hawaii* (1966), *Thoroughly Modern Millie* (1967), *10* (1979), *S.O.B.* (1981), *Victor/Victoria* (1982), *Duet for One* (1986), *The Princess Diaries* (2001)

Notable Awards: Grammy Award, Best Recording for Children (1965); Academy Award, Best Actress (1965); Golden Globe Awards, Best Actress—Motion Picture, Musical/Comedy (1965, 1966, 1983); British Academy of Film and Television Arts (BAFTA) Award, Outstanding British Contribution to Cinema (1989); American Film Institute, Lifetime Achievement Award (2022)

CHRISTIAN BALE

Christian Bale was 13 when he starred in his first movie, the 1987 film *Empire of the Sun*. He played a young boy who was separated from his parents during World War II (1939–1945). Bale continued to get roles in popular movies, such as *Newsies* and *Little Women*.

COMMITMENT TO THE ROLE

As an adult, Bale gained widespread fame for playing Batman in *The Dark Knight* trilogy. He's also known for playing complex characters and diving headfirst into his roles. In 2000, Bale

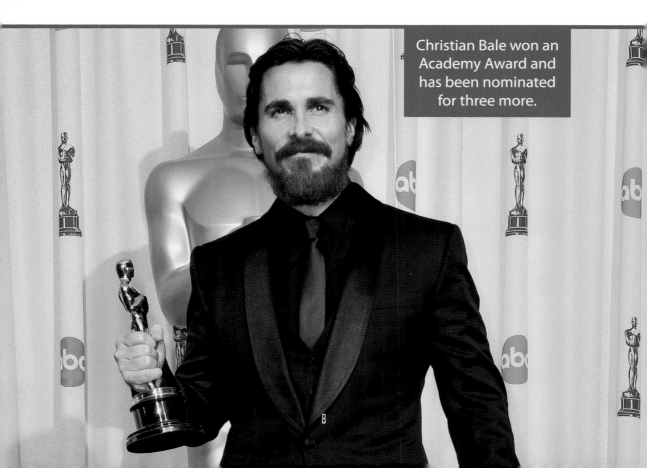

Christian Bale won an Academy Award and has been nominated for three more.

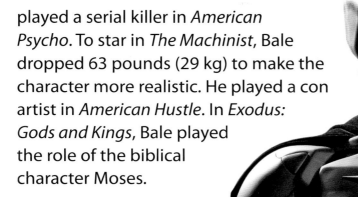

played a serial killer in *American Psycho*. To star in *The Machinist*, Bale dropped 63 pounds (29 kg) to make the character more realistic. He played a con artist in *American Hustle*. In *Exodus: Gods and Kings*, Bale played the role of the biblical character Moses.

Bale's Batman was more serious than earlier versions of the character.

AT A GLANCE

Notable Films: *Little Women* (1994), *American Psycho* (2000), *The Dark Knight* trilogy (2005, 2008, 2012), *The Prestige* (2006), *3:10 to Yuma* (2007), *The Fighter* (2010), *American Hustle* (2013), *The Big Short* (2015), *Vice* (2018), *Ford v Ferrari* (2019)

Notable Awards: Golden Globe Awards, Best Supporting Actor—Motion Picture (2011), Best Actor—Motion Picture, Musical/Comedy (2019); Academy Award, Best Supporting Actor (2011)

ANTONIO BANDERAS

ntonio Banderas began acting with the Spanish National Theater. His first movie was *Laberinto de Pasiones* (*Labyrinth of Passion*) in 1982. In 1989, Banderas moved to Hollywood to further his career. He didn't know much English at that time. He learned his lines phonetically, or by sounding out the words. He also took classes to improve his English skills. Banderas's first English-language movie was *The Mambo Kings*. He appeared in many films in the 1990s and 2000s. Banderas also voice acted in the *Shrek* sequels. He played the cat character Puss in Boots.

Antonio Banderas won the Goya Award for Best Lead Actor for his role in *Pain and Glory*.

AT A GLANCE

Notable Films: *The Mambo Kings* (1992), *Philadelphia* (1993), *Desperado* (1995), *Evita* (1996), *The Mask of Zorro* (1998), *Once upon a Time in Mexico* (2003), *The Skin I Live In* (2011), *Pain and Glory* (2019)

Notable Awards: European Film Award, European Actor (2019); Cannes Film Festival, Best Actor (2019); Goya Award, Best Lead Actor (2020)

DID YOU KNOW?

The Goya Awards honor the best of Spanish filmmaking. The Spanish Academy of Motion Picture Arts and Sciences presents the awards each year.

JAVIER BARDEM

Javier Bardem was born in Spain on March 1, 1969. At age six, he starred in one episode of the Spanish television show *El Picaro* (*The Scoundrel*). Bardem continued to get roles in various television shows as a teenager. It wasn't until the 1992 film *Jamón Jamón* (*Ham Ham*) that he gained more popularity. He continued to be cast in Spanish films, and his first film in English was *Before Night Falls* in 2000. Bardem won an Academy Award for playing an assassin in *No Country for Old Men*.

Javier Bardem played Anton Chigurh in *No Country for Old Men*. The killer is known for being strange, mysterious, and cold.

AT A GLANCE

Notable Films: *Before Night Falls* (2000), *The Sea Inside* (2004), *Collateral* (2004), *No Country for Old Men* (2007), *Love in the Time of Cholera* (2007), *Vicki Cristina Barcelona* (2008), *Biutiful* (2010), *Skyfall* (2012), *To the Wonder* (2012), *Dune* (2021)

Notable Awards: Goya Awards, Best Lead Actor (1996, 2003, 2005, 2011, 2022); European Film Awards, Best Actor (1997), European Actor (2004); Academy Award, Best Supporting Actor (2008); Golden Globe Award, Best Supporting Actor—Motion Picture (2008); BAFTA Award, Best Supporting Actor (2008); Cannes Film Festival, Best Actor (2010)

Angela Bassett was in high school when she saw the play *Of Mice and Men*. She decided then that she wanted to act. In the mid-1980s, Bassett starred in a Broadway play, *Ma Rainey's Black Bottom*. During this time, she also began acting in television shows. These included small roles in *The Cosby Show* and *Spenser: For Hire*.

STRONG FEMALE ROLES

Bassett is known for her roles featuring Black women from history. She played civil rights activists Betty Shabazz and Rosa Parks in the films *Malcolm X* and *The Rosa Parks Story*, respectively. Bassett's role as singer Tina Turner in *What's Love Got to Do with It?* brought her fame.

Angela Bassett and her husband run a production company that promotes Black stories.

Another notable role for Bassett was playing Ramonda in *Black Panther*. She continued with the role in *Avengers: Endgame* and *Black Panther: Wakanda Forever*. She received an Academy Award nomination for her role in *Black Panther: Wakanda Forever*.

AT A GLANCE

Notable Films: *Malcolm X* (1992), *What's Love Got to Do with It* (1993), *Waiting to Exhale* (1995), *How Stella Got Her Groove Back* (1998), *Music of the Heart* (1999), *Sunshine State* (2002), *The Rosa Parks Story* (2002), *Akeelah and the Bee* (2006), *Black Panther* (2018), *Black Panther: Wakanda Forever* (2022)

Notable Awards: Golden Globe Awards, Best Actress—Motion Picture, Musical/Comedy (1994), Best Supporting Actress—Motion Picture (2023)

Bassett's character in *Black Panther*, Ramonda, is the queen of Wakanda.

Kathy Bates moved to New York City in 1970. She had success on the stage. Bates was nominated for a Tony Award for her role in the play *'Night, Mother* in the early 1980s.

DIVERSE CHARACTERS

Bates achieved widespread fame for her role in the movie *Misery*. In the film, she played a psychotic, obsessed fan who kidnaps a novelist. Bates won a Golden Globe and an Academy Award for the role.

Throughout her acting career, Bates has played a variety of characters. In *Fried Green Tomatoes*, she was cast as a housewife living in the South. In *Titanic*, Bates played

Kathy Bates often plays strong, outspoken female characters.

DID YOU KNOW?

The Tony Awards are given to celebrate excellence in the theater. They are named for actor, director, and producer Antoinette Perry. The Tony Awards were first given in 1947.

Notable Films: *Come Back to the 5 & Dime, Jimmy Dean, Jimmy Dean* (1982), *Misery* (1990), *Fried Green Tomatoes* (1991), *Dolores Claiborne* (1995), *Titanic* (1997), *Primary Colors* (1998), *About Schmidt* (2002), *Revolutionary Road* (2008), *The Day the Earth Stood Still* (2008), *Richard Jewell* (2019)

Notable Awards: Academy Award, Best Actress (1991); Golden Globe Awards, Best Actress—Motion Picture, Drama (1991), Best Supporting Actress—Television (1997); Screen Actors Guild Awards, Outstanding Performance by a Female Actor in a TV Movie or Miniseries (1997), Outstanding Performance by a Female Actor in a Supporting Role (1999)

the vocal socialite Molly Brown. She has also had roles in romantic comedies, a sports drama, and a biographical film. In addition to acting, Bates has directed television shows. These include *Dash and Lilly*, *Six Feet Under*, and *NYPD Blue*.

Bates is known for playing characters on the television series *American Horror Story*.

15

HALLE BERRY

Halle Berry's parts in the films *Jungle Fever* and *Boomerang* led to her rise in fame in the early 1990s. Berry is known for taking on tough roles and morphing into her characters. For instance, to prepare for her role as a woman addicted to cocaine in *Jungle Fever*, Berry did not bathe for two weeks. Her role in *Monster's Ball* earned her an Academy Award for Best Actress. Berry was the first Black woman to win the award in that category.

Halle Berry was only the seventh Black actress nominated for an Academy Award.

AT A GLANCE

Notable Films: *Jungle Fever* (1991), *Losing Isaiah* (1993), *Bulworth* (1998), *Introducing Dorothy Dandridge* (1999), *X-Men* (2000), *Monster's Ball* (2001), *Die Another Day* (2002), *Gothika* (2003), *The Call* (2013), *Bruised* (2020)

Notable Awards: Golden Globe Award, Best Actress—Limited Series, Anthology Series, or Television Motion Picture (2000); Emmy Award, Outstanding Lead Actress in a Miniseries or a Movie (2000); Academy Award, Best Actress (2002)

CATE BLANCHETT

ate Blanchett began acting in theater productions such as *Oleanna* in 1993. In that role, Blanchett played a college student who said she was harassed by a teacher. The first movie role that pushed Blanchett to stardom was her portrayal of Queen Elizabeth I in *Elizabeth*. She won a Golden Globe and received an Academy Award

In 2007, Cate Blanchett played Queen Elizabeth again in *Elizabeth: The Golden Age.*

nomination. Critics also praised Blanchett for her role as the elf queen Galadriel in the *Lord of the Rings* movie series. She won Academy Awards for her roles in *The Aviator* and *Blue Jasmine*.

AT A GLANCE

Notable Films: *Elizabeth* (1998), *The Talented Mr. Ripley* (1999), *Lord of the Rings* series (2001, 2002, 2003), *The Aviator* (2004), *Notes on a Scandal* (2006), *I'm Not There* (2007), *Blue Jasmine* (2013), *Carol* (2015), *Nightmare Alley* (2021), *Tár* (2022)

Notable Awards: Golden Globe Awards, Best Actress—Motion Picture, Drama (1999, 2014, 2023), Best Supporting Actress—Motion Picture (2008); BAFTA Awards, Best Actress (1999, 2014, 2023), Best Performance by an Actress in a Supporting Role (2005); Academy Awards, Best Supporting Actress (2005), Best Actress (2014)

During World War I (1914–1918), Humphrey Bogart served in the US Navy. Afterward, he began acting in plays in New York City. He found success on Broadway, particularly with his role in *The Petrified Forest* in 1935, where he played a gangster. A year later, Bogart was cast as the same character but this time on the big screen.

NOBLE AND TOUGH

With his roles in *High Sierra* and *The Maltese Falcon*, Bogart's fame soared. He also starred in *Casablanca*, playing the owner of a cabaret in Morocco during World War II. Bogart won an Academy Award for Best Actor for his

Humphrey Bogart starred in a television adaptation of *The Petrified Forest*. He acted alongside his wife, Lauren Bacall.

Notable Films: *The Maltese Falcon* (1941), *Casablanca* (1943), *To Have and Have Not* (1945), *The Big Sleep* (1946), *The Treasure of the Sierra Madre* (1948), *Key Largo* (1948), *In a Lonely Place* (1950), *The African Queen* (1951), *Sabrina* (1954), *The Caine Mutiny* (1954)
Notable Awards: Academy Award, Best Actor (1952)

role in *The African Queen*. In that movie, he played the captain of a riverboat.

Bogart was a popular actor throughout the 1940s and 1950s. He appeared in a wide range of genres, from musicals to crime dramas. He often played characters who were tough but noble. In 1999, the American Film Institute named Bogart the top male film star of the 1900s.

Bogart wore a fedora and trench coat in *Casablanca*. The look became iconic.

In high school, Chadwick Boseman played basketball. After a teammate died, Boseman wrote his first stage play. He fell in love with storytelling. Boseman graduated from Howard University in 2000, where he focused his studies on directing. He then looked for writing, directing, and acting jobs in New York City theaters. He also landed some television roles.

A SUPERHERO AND A STAR

In *Captain America: Civil War*, Boseman played the character of T'Challa, a superhero known as the Black Panther. Boseman took on the role of T'Challa again in *Black Panther*, *Avengers: Infinity War*, and *Avengers: Endgame*.

Boseman tackled more than superhero roles. He played young Thurgood Marshall, the first Black member of the US Supreme Court, in the film *Marshall*. Boseman also acted as a musician in

Chadwick Boseman's first major role was portraying baseball player Jackie Robinson in *42*.

AT A GLANCE

Notable Films: *42* (2013), *Get On Up* (2014), *Draft Day* (2014), *Captain America: Civil War* (2016), *Marshall* (2017), *Black Panther* (2018), *Avengers: Infinity War* (2018), *Avengers: Endgame* (2019), *21 Bridges* (2019), *Ma Rainey's Black Bottom* (2020), *Da 5 Bloods* (2020)

Notable Awards: Golden Globe Award, Best Actor—Motion Picture, Drama (2021); Screen Actors Guild Award, Outstanding Performance by a Male Actor in a Leading Role (2021)

Ma Rainey's Black Bottom. Boseman died of cancer in 2020. He was nominated for an Academy Award for *Ma Rainey's Black Bottom* after his death.

After Boseman's death, his character T'Challa was not recast for the then-upcoming movie *Black Panther: Wakanda Forever*.

In 1943, at age 19, Marlon Brando moved from the Midwest to New York City. He enrolled in acting classes. Soon he was appearing in Broadway plays. Brando had so much success on the stage that critics in New York called him "Broadway's most promising actor."

FROM PLAYS TO FILMS

In 1947, Brando played the emotionally explosive character Stanley Kowalski in the Broadway play *A Streetcar Named Desire*. He landed the role again for the 1951 movie of the

DID YOU KNOW?

Brando refused to accept the Academy Award for Best Actor for his role in *The Godfather*. He was protesting how American Indians were portrayed in the media and treated by the US government.

A Streetcar Named Desire won four Academy Awards. Marlon Brando's nomination was one of eight.

same name. He was nominated for an Academy Award.

Three years later, Brando's role in *On the Waterfront* cemented his popularity. It also won him an Academy Award for Best Actor. During the 1960s, his career slowed after starring in several unsuccessful movies. Brando also gained a reputation for being a difficult and demanding actor. His role playing a crime boss in *The Godfather* won him another Academy Award.

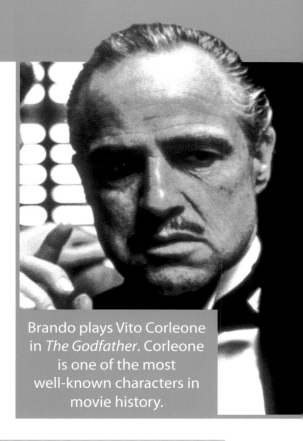

Brando plays Vito Corleone in *The Godfather*. Corleone is one of the most well-known characters in movie history.

AT A GLANCE

Notable Films: *A Streetcar Named Desire* (1951), *Viva Zapata!* (1952), *Julius Caesar* (1953), *On the Waterfront* (1954), *The Fugitive Kind* (1960), *One-Eyed Jacks* (1961), *Mutiny on the Bounty* (1962), *The Chase* (1966), *The Godfather* (1972), *Apocalypse Now* (1979)

Notable Awards: Cannes Film Festival, Best Actor (1952); BAFTA Awards, Best Foreign Actor (1953, 1954, 1955); Academy Awards, Best Actor (1955, 1973); Golden Globe Awards, Best Actor—Motion Picture, Drama (1955, 1973), World Film Favorites (1956, 1973, 1974); Emmy Award, Outstanding Supporting Actor in a Limited Series or a Special (1979)

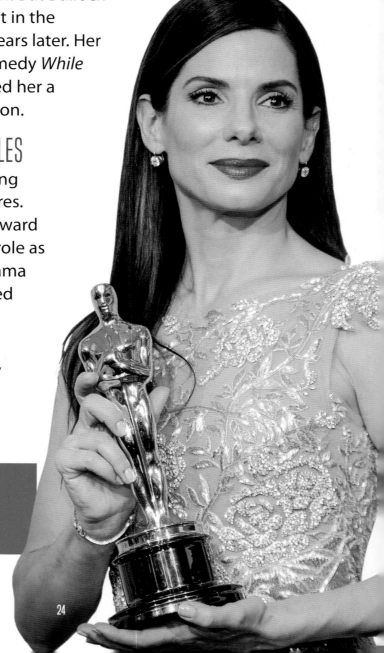

S andra Bullock's first film role was in the 1987 movie *Hangmen*. But Bullock gained fame for her part in the popular thriller *Speed* years later. Her role in the romantic comedy *While You Were Sleeping* earned her a Golden Globe nomination.

TACKLING DIFFERENT ROLES

Bullock has tackled acting roles in a variety of genres. She won an Academy Award for Best Actress for her role as a mom in the sports drama *The Blind Side*. She played another strong mother role in *Extremely Loud & Incredibly Close*. In 2013, she and actor George Clooney starred in *Gravity*. It is a story

Sandra Bullock's Oscar for *The Blind Side* was her first Academy Award nomination and win.

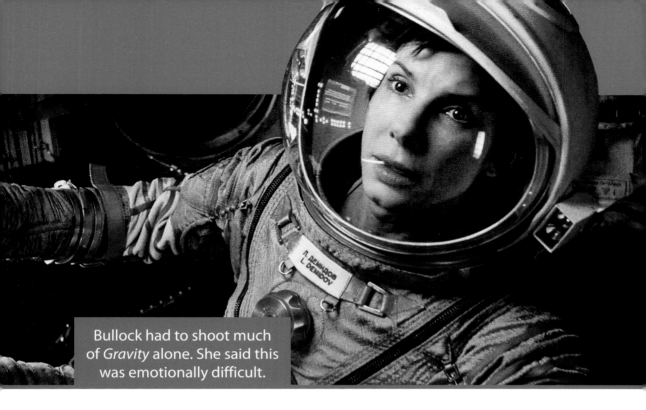

Bullock had to shoot much of *Gravity* alone. She said this was emotionally difficult.

about astronauts whose spacecraft has been destroyed. In 2018, Bullock played a jewelry thief in *Ocean's 8*. She took on another comedy role in *The Lost City*, playing a kidnapped romance writer.

AT A GLANCE

Notable Films: *The Thing Called Love* (1993), *Demolition Man* (1993), *Speed* (1994), *While You Were Sleeping* (1995), *Infamous* (2006), *The Lake House* (2006), *The Blind Side* (2009), *Gravity* (2013), *The Heat* (2013), *The Lost City* (2022)

Notable Awards: Academy Award, Best Actress (2010); Golden Globe Award, Best Actress—Motion Picture, Drama (2010); Screen Actors Guild Award, Outstanding Performance by a Female Actor in a Leading Role (2010)

NICOLAS CAGE

Nicolas Cage's name at birth was Nicolas Kim Coppola. Cage's uncle is the famous film director Francis Ford Coppola. He wanted to distinguish himself from his uncle. So he adopted the stage name Nicolas Cage when he began acting.

Cage landed a film role in *Fast Times at Ridgemont High* in 1982. He won a Best Actor Academy Award for *Leaving Last Vegas*. Cage is often busy. Sometimes he makes more than five films in one year. Many of Cage's roles have been in action films or big-budget summer films.

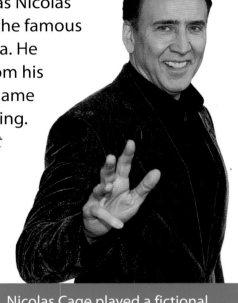

Nicolas Cage played a fictional version of himself in *The Unbearable Weight of Massive Talent* in 2022.

AT A GLANCE

Notable Films: *Birdy* (1984), *Moonstruck* (1987), *Raising Arizona* (1987), *Honeymoon in Vegas* (1992), *Leaving Las Vegas* (1995), *The Rock* (1996), *Adaptation* (2002), *National Treasure* (2004), *Pig* (2021), *The Unbearable Weight of Massive Talent* (2022)

Notable Awards: Academy Award, Best Actor (1996); Golden Globe Award, Best Actor—Motion Picture, Drama (1996); Screen Actors Guild Award, Outstanding Performance by a Male Actor in a Leading Role (1996)

JIM CARREY

As a child, Jim Carrey liked making funny faces in the mirror. He had a knack for impressions too. At age 15, Carrey got a job doing stand-up comedy in a club. By age 19, he had moved to Hollywood and soon landed film roles. Some of his early comedy hits were *Ace Ventura: Pet Detective*, *The Mask*, and *Dumb and Dumber*. Carrey is known for starring in comedies. But he has also played more serious roles, such as a police officer investigating a murder in the movie *Dark Crimes*.

Jim Carrey was known for his physical comedy and exaggerated performance in *Ace Ventura*.

AT A GLANCE

Notable Films: *Ace Ventura: Pet Detective* (1994), *Dumb and Dumber* (1994), *Ace Ventura: When Nature Calls* (1995), *The Cable Guy* (1996), *Liar, Liar* (1997), *The Truman Show* (1998), *Man on the Moon* (1999), *Bruce Almighty* (2003), *Eternal Sunshine of the Spotless Mind* (2004), *Dark Crimes* (2016), *Sonic the Hedgehog* (2020)

Notable Awards: Golden Globe Awards, Best Actor—Motion Picture, Drama (1999), Best Actor—Motion Picture, Musical/Comedy (2000)

TIMOTHÉE CHALAMET

Timothée Chalamet won a Film Independent Spirit Award for Best Male Lead for his role in *Call Me by Your Name*.

Timothée Chalamet was still in high school when he landed his first film roles. These were for the 2014 movies *Men, Women & Children* and *Interstellar*. He was also acting on television shows such as *Law & Order*, *Royal Pains*, and *Homeland*.

A YOUNG AWARD-WINNER

Chalamet's 2017 films, *Lady Bird* and *Call Me by Your Name*, were praised by film critics and movie audiences. He was nominated for Best Actor at the Academy Awards for his role in *Call Me by Your Name*, in which he plays the lead role. At age 23, Chalamet was the youngest actor in 80 years to receive a Best Actor nomination. He was also chosen for the lead role in the epic science-fiction movie *Dune*. Chalamet received positive reviews for his part in that film, which won six Academy Awards.

Chalamet was in his early twenties when he starred in *Dune*. He played teenager Paul Atreides.

JACKIE CHAN

Jackie Chan was born on April 7, 1954, in Hong Kong, China. As a child, he was trained in martial arts, singing, and acrobatics. As a young adult, Chan used his martial arts skills to land roles in kung fu movies in Hong Kong. He often did his own stunts, breaking some bones in the process.

Jackie Chan, *left*, starred beside Jaden Smith in *The Karate Kid*.

Chan had acted in more than 200 movies when he won his honorary Academy Award.

BREAKING INTO HOLLYWOOD

Chan's film *Rumble in the Bronx* was his breakthrough film in the United States. A few years later, his movie *Rush Hour* was also a hit. In the early 2000s, Chan was making movies in both the United States and Hong Kong. His popular US films included the 2010 remake of *The Karate Kid* and the *Kung Fu Panda* movie series. Chan was the first Chinese actor to receive an honorary Academy Award for his distinctive international career.

AT A GLANCE

Notable Movies: *Drunken Master* (1978), *Project A* (1983), *Police Story* (1985), *Dragons Forever* (1988), *Supercop* (1992), *Crime Story* (1993), *The Legend of Drunken Master* (1994), *Rumble in the Bronx* (1995), *Rush Hour* (1998), *Shanghai Noon* (2000), *Kung Fu Panda* series (2008, 2011, 2016), *The Karate Kid* (2010)

Notable Awards: Academy Award, Honorary Award (2016)

CHARLIE CHAPLIN

Charlie Chaplin was a comedian who performed onstage and in films. He was born on April 16, 1889, in England. By his early twenties, Chaplin was getting roles in comedy films. He created the iconic Tramp character. This was a mischievous man who was often a misfit. The character was also resilient and always looking forward to new adventures. When playing the Tramp, Chaplin wore baggy pants, a jacket that was too tight, floppy shoes, and a tiny mustache. Audiences loved Chaplin's Tramp.

FROM SILENT TO TALKIES

While gaining experience as an actor, Chaplin

SILENT FILMS

Silent films were made from around 1891 to 1927. Filmmakers told a story through the actors' actions and facial expressions. These films often had a music accompaniment that played during the film, but there were no spoken parts by the actors. Some of the most famous silent films were *The Ten Commandments* (1923), *The Big Parade* (1925), and *Sunrise* (1927). The first talkie appeared around 1927. Experts consider *The Jazz Singer* to be the first successful talkie.

Charlie Chaplin's derby hat was part of his iconic look as the Tramp.

Chaplin, *right*, directed *The Great Dictator* in addition to starring in the film.

began directing and producing films too. He won his first Academy Award for his role in *The Circus*. His early films were silent movies, or movies that didn't have any talking. But as time passed and technology advanced, people began to make sound movies, or talkies. *The Great Dictator*, produced in 1940, was Chaplin's first sound movie.

AT A GLANCE

Notable Movies: *The Tramp* (1915), *A Dog's Life* (1918), *The Kid* (1921), *The Gold Rush* (1925), *The Circus* (1928), *City Lights* (1931), *Modern Times* (1936), *The Great Dictator* (1940), *Monsieur Verdoux* (1947), *Limelight* (1952), *A King in New York* (1957)

Notable Awards: Academy Awards, Honorary Award (1929, 1972); BAFTA Award, Academy Fellowship (1976); New York Film Critics Circle Award, Best Actor (1940)

DON CHEADLE

Don Cheadle is a talented musician in addition to being an actor.

Don Cheadle studied acting in college. He appeared in his first film, *Moving Violations*, while he was still a student. Cheadle had roles in the television shows *Hill Street Blues*, *Night Court*, and *Picket Fences*. Critics took note of his performance in the 1995 film *Devil in a Blue Dress*. He earned an Academy Award nomination for Best Actor for *Hotel Rwanda*, a film set during the Rwandan genocide of 1994.

A SUPERHERO AND A DIRECTOR

Cheadle also played a superhero named James Rhodes, or War Machine, in the *Avengers* series. In 2015, he cowrote, directed, and starred in *Miles Ahead*. This film told the story of jazz musician Miles Davis. Cheadle has taken roles in both comedies and dramas. He is known for portraying a strong, quiet intensity in his roles.

AT A GLANCE

Notable Films: *Devil in a Blue Dress* (1995), *Boogie Nights* (1997), *Traffic* (2000), *Ocean's Eleven* (2001), *Hotel Rwanda* (2004), *Crash* (2004), *Flight* (2012), *Captain America: Civil War* (2016), *Avengers: Infinity War* (2018), *Avengers: Endgame* (2019)

Notable Awards: Golden Globe Awards, Best Supporting Actor—Television (1999), Best Television Actor—Musical/Comedy (2013); Grammy Awards, Best Compilation Soundtrack for Visual Media (2017), Best Spoken Word Album (2022)

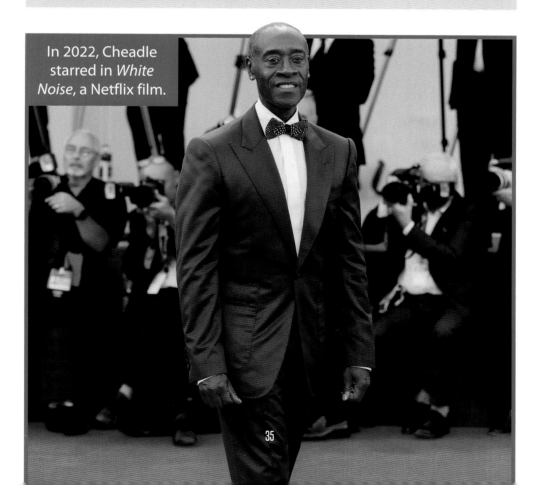

In 2022, Cheadle starred in *White Noise*, a Netflix film.

GEORGE CLOONEY

George Clooney became popular with audiences while playing a doctor in the hit television series *ER*. After this success, he began starring in movies. Clooney is known for his ability to adapt to many different roles. He played an escaped convict in the movie *O Brother, Where Art Thou?* and received a Golden Globe Award. He played a thief in the *Ocean's Eleven* movie series. In *Syriana*, Clooney acted as a CIA agent. His performance in that film earned him his first Academy Award for Best Supporting Actor.

George Clooney, *blue shirt*, was part of the *ER* cast for five seasons.

Clooney has been nominated for six Academy Awards in addition to his two wins.

WRITING AND DIRECTING

Clooney also had success as a film director and screenwriter. He cowrote, directed, and starred in the 2014 film *The Monuments Men*. Clooney also produced and starred in the film *Michael Clayton*. This role earned him a Best Actor Academy Award nomination. For his work as an actor, writer, producer, and director, Clooney received the Golden Globe Cecil B. DeMille Award. This is given to people who have made exceptional contributions to the entertainment industry.

GARY COOPER

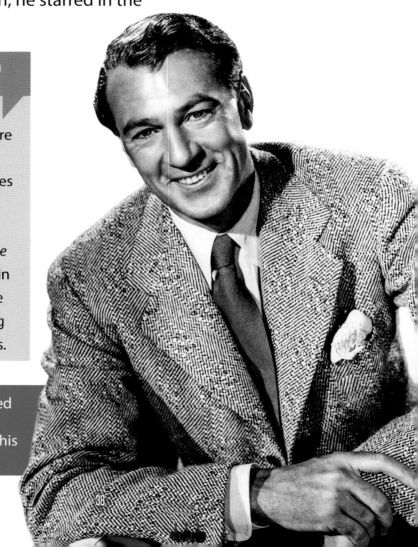

Gary Cooper was born on May 7, 1901, in Helena, Montana. He got his start in movies as a stunt rider and cowboy extra. Cooper became popular with audiences after starring in the 1929 film *The Virginian*. Cooper often played a somewhat shy, quiet hero who did not seek fame for himself. Cooper also played baseball player Lou Gehrig in the film *Pride of the Yankees*. In addition, he starred in the

DID YOU KNOW?

The term *Westerns* refers to a story genre that is set in the western United States around the mid- to late 1800s. The first Western film was *The Great Train Robbery* in 1903. Westerns were most popular during the 1940s and 1950s.

Gary Cooper acted in more than 100 films during his 38-year career.

movies *For Whom the Bell Tolls* and *A Farewell to Arms*.

BEST ACTOR AWARDS

Cooper won the Best Actor Academy Award twice. His first Academy Award came for his part in *Sergeant York*. His second was for his role in *High Noon*. Many critics think that Cooper's performance as the town marshal in *High Noon* is his best acting.

Cooper was the second pick for his role in *High Noon*. But the choice paid off.

AT A GLANCE

Notable Films: *Design for Living* (1933), *Mr. Deeds Goes to Town* (1936), *Ball of Fire* (1941), *Sergeant York* (1941), *Meet John Doe* (1941), *The Pride of the Yankees* (1942), *High Noon* (1952), *Friendly Persuasion* (1956), *Love in the Afternoon* (1957), *Man of the West* (1958)

Notable Awards: New York Film Critics Circle Award, Best Actor (1941); Academy Awards, Best Actor (1942, 1953), Honorary Award (1961); Golden Globe Award, Best Actor—Drama (1953)

Joan Crawford was a popular actress in the early to mid-1900s. She first took to the stage as a dancer, working in nightclubs and Broadway musicals. Crawford eventually landed dancing roles in films such as *Our Dancing Daughters* and *Dancing Lady*. Along the way, Crawford shifted from dancing into acting roles. She often played glamorous characters in movies. Her first talking film was *Untamed* in 1929.

MEMORABLE ROLES

Crawford won an Academy Award for her part in *Mildred Pierce* in 1946. In this role, Crawford played a determined waitress who becomes the owner of a chain of restaurants. The 1962 film *Whatever Happened to Baby Jane?* was another big success for Crawford. In that movie, she played a former actress who is terrorized by her younger sister.

Many of Joan Crawford's early roles were in silent films.

AT A GLANCE

Notable Films: *Grand Hotel* (1932), *The Women* (1939), *Mildred Pierce* (1945), *Humoresque* (1946), *Possessed* (1947), *Sudden Fear* (1952), *Johnny Guitar* (1954), *The Best of Everything* (1959), *Whatever Happened to Baby Jane?* (1962), *Strait-Jacket* (1964)

Notable Awards: National Board of Review, Best Actress (1945); Academy Award, Best Actress (1946); Golden Globe Award, Cecil B. DeMille Award (1970)

Crawford received her Academy Award for *Mildred Pierce* while she was ill. She was given her award in bed.

TOM CRUISE

Tom Cruise landed his first film role before he was 20. Cruise had a string of popular movies in the 1980s. In 1983, he played the role of a high school senior in the popular film *Risky Business*. In 1986, he starred as a Navy jet pilot in the well-known film *Top Gun*. Three years later, he received his first of four Academy Award nominations for his role as a Vietnam War (1954–1975) veteran in *Born on the Fourth of July*.

ACTION MOVIES AND STUNTS

In the 1990s, Cruise played a wide range of characters. He played a vampire in

Tom Cruise played a character named Maverick in *Top Gun*. He played the same role in *Top Gun: Maverick*.

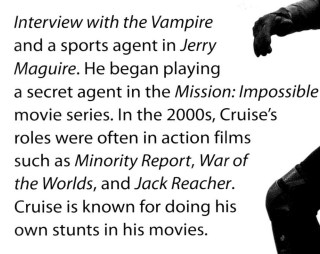

Interview with the Vampire and a sports agent in *Jerry Maguire*. He began playing a secret agent in the *Mission: Impossible* movie series. In the 2000s, Cruise's roles were often in action films such as *Minority Report*, *War of the Worlds*, and *Jack Reacher*. Cruise is known for doing his own stunts in his movies.

Safety harnesses make many of Cruise's stunts possible.

AT A GLANCE

Notable Films: *Risky Business* (1983), *Top Gun* (1986), *Born on the Fourth of July* (1989), *Jerry Maguire* (1996), *Eyes Wide Shut* (1999), *Magnolia* (1999), *Minority Report* (2002), *Collateral* (2004), *Mission: Impossible—Fallout* (2018), *Top Gun: Maverick* (2022)

Notable Awards: Golden Globe Awards, Best Actor—Motion Picture, Drama (1990), Best Actor—Motion Picture, Musical/Comedy (1997), Best Supporting Actor—Motion Picture (2000); National Board of Review, Best Actor (1996); Cannes Film Festival, Honorary Golden Palm (2022)

PENÉLOPE CRUZ

Penélope Cruz was born on April 28, 1974, in Spain. She trained as a dancer and then went to New York City to study theater. At age 15, Cruz began appearing in music videos and Spanish television shows.

FILMS IN SPANISH AND ENGLISH

Cruz starred in the movie *Belle Epoque* (*The Age of Beauty*) in 1992, which won an Academy Award for Best Foreign Film. Her first English-language film was *Talk of Angels* in 1998. That role opened more doors for her in Hollywood. Cruz continued acting in both English- and Spanish-language films. She made several movies with

Penélope Cruz has been nominated for three Academy Awards in addition to her win.

AT A GLANCE

Notable Films: *Jamón Jamón* (1992), *Open Your Eyes* (1997), *All about My Mother* (1999), *Volver* (2006), *Vicky Cristina Barcelona* (2008), *Broken Embraces* (2009), *Nine* (2009), *Ma Ma* (2015), *Pain and Glory* (2019), *Parallel Mothers* (2021)

Notable Awards: Goya Awards, Best Lead Actress (1999, 2007), Best Supporting Actress (2009); Cannes Film Festival, Best Actress (2006); National Board of Review, Best Supporting Actress (2008); New York Film Critics Circle Award, Best Supporting Actress (2008); Academy Award, Best Supporting Actress (2009); BAFTA Award, Best Supporting Actress (2009); Los Angeles Film Critics Association Awards, Best Supporting Actress (2008), Best Actress (2021)

Spanish director Pedro Almodóvar, including *All about My Mother*, *Broken Embraces*, and *Pain and Glory*. Cruz received an Academy Award for Best Supporting Actress for her work in *Vicky Cristina Barcelona*, where she played the main character's ex-wife.

Cruz starred in *Todos lo Saben* (*Everybody Knows*) alongside her husband, Javier Bardem.

JAMIE LEE CURTIS

Jamie Lee Curtis has acted in seven *Halloween* movies.

Jamie Lee Curtis's popularity soared when she played a babysitter in the 1978 horror film *Halloween*. She appeared in more horror films afterward. Her work in this genre earned her the nickname "Scream Queen."

MOVING INTO COMEDIES

Curtis also appeared in several popular comedy films, such as *Trading Places*, *Perfect*, and *A Fish Called Wanda*. In 1990,

Curtis won her first Golden Globe for her part in the television show *Anything but Love*. She won a second Golden Globe after starring in the popular action-comedy film *True Lies*. In that movie, she played the wife of a spy.

In 2019, Curtis joined a cast of all-star actors for the popular detective mystery *Knives Out*. Three years later, Curtis starred in *Everything Everywhere All at Once* as a tax inspector. The performance gave Curtis her first Academy Award.

Curtis acknowledged her parents in her Academy Award acceptance speech.

AT A GLANCE

Notable Films: *Halloween* (1978), *The Fog* (1980), *Trading Places* (1983), *A Fish Called Wanda* (1988), *My Girl* (1991), *True Lies* (1994), *Freaky Friday* (2003), *Knives Out* (2019), *Everything Everywhere All at Once* (2022)

Notable Awards: BAFTA Award, Best Supporting Actress (1984); Golden Globe Awards, Best Television Actress—Musical/Comedy (1990), Best Actress—Motion Picture, Musical/Comedy (1995); Screen Actors Guild Award, Female Actor in a Supporting Role (2023); Academy Award, Best Supporting Actress (2023)

Bette Davis landed her first roles on Broadway. She appeared in *The Earth Between* and *Broken Dishes*. Her strong performances onstage caught Hollywood's attention. She began appearing in films. Davis received critical praise for her role in the 1932 movie *The Man Who Played God*. In 1934, Davis played a mean, unsympathetic character in *Of Human Bondage*. Two years later, she won an Academy Award for her role in *Dangerous*. In that film, she played an actress with a substance use disorder. Davis earned a second Academy Award for her

HOLLYWOOD'S STUDIO SYSTEM

During the 1930s and 1940s, most movies were created by five big film studios. These were Metro-Goldwin-Mayer, Warner Bros., Paramount, Fox, and RKO. Everyone who worked on the movies, including the actors, were under contract to work for a specific studio. The studios also owned the movie theaters where their movies were shown.

Bette Davis was born on April 5, 1908, in Lowell, Massachusetts.

Davis starred in *Dangerous* with Franchot Tone.

performance in *Jezebel*. In that movie, Davis played a determined woman living in the South.

A LONG, SUCCESSFUL CAREER

Davis had a long career. She featured in approximately 100 films. She received Academy Award nominations ten times. She won the award twice. In 1977, the American Film Institute gave her a Life Achievement Award. She was the first woman to receive the award.

VIOLA DAVIS

Viola Davis is famous for her regal presence both on the stage and on-screen.

In 1996, Viola Davis starred in the Broadway play *Seven Guitars*. Her performance was powerful. She received a nomination for a Tony Award. The same year, she appeared in her first movie, *The Substance of Fire*. In 2001, Davis earned her first Tony Award for her work in *King Hedley II*. In that play, she portrayed a woman who wanted to get an abortion.

WINNING AWARDS

Davis's roles in the films *Doubt* and *The Help* earned her praise from movie critics. She was nominated for an Academy Award for both of those movies. Davis won her first Academy Award for her performance in *Fences*.

AT A GLANCE

Notable Films: *Doubt* (2008), *Eat Pray Love* (2010), *The Help* (2011), *Won't Back Down* (2012), *Prisoners* (2013), *Get On Up* (2014), *Fences* (2016), *Widows* (2018), *Ma Rainey's Black Bottom* (2020), *The Woman King* (2022)

Notable Awards: Tony Awards, Best Actress (2001, 2010); Screen Actors Guild Awards, Outstanding Performance by a Female Actor in a Leading Role (2012, 2021), Outstanding Performance by a Female Actor in a Drama Series (2015, 2016), Outstanding Performance by a Female Actor in a Supporting Role (2017); Emmy Award, Outstanding Lead Actress in a Drama Series (2015); Academy Award, Best Supporting Actress (2017); Golden Globe Award, Best Supporting Actress—Motion Picture (2017)

In addition, Davis won an Emmy Award for her part in the television show *How to Get Away with Murder*. In 2023, Davis earned a Grammy Award for her audiobook *Finding Me*. She is one of the few artists who have won an Emmy, Grammy, Oscar, and Tony (EGOT).

Davis holds up her Academy Award, which she won in 2017.

DANIEL DAY-LEWIS

Daniel Day-Lewis grew up in England and began acting while still in school. Day-Lewis spent several years performing with theater companies. He landed his first movie role at age 13. As an adult, his first movie appearance was in the 1982 film *Gandhi*, where he played the small role of a street bully.

GROWING FAME

Day-Lewis's performances in movies such as *My Beautiful Laundrette* and *The Unbearable Lightness of Being* brought him fame as an actor. His role as an artist with cerebral palsy in *My Left Foot* earned him the Best Actor Academy Award. Known for

Daniel Day-Lewis, *left*, stands with other Academy Award winners in 2013.

deeply immersing himself in his roles, Day-Lewis learned to paint with his left foot to prepare himself for playing the part.

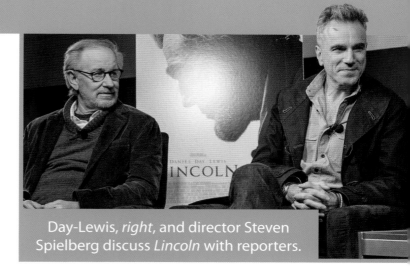

Day-Lewis, *right*, and director Steven Spielberg discuss *Lincoln* with reporters.

Day-Lewis earned his second Academy Award for the film *There Will Be Blood*. His role as Abraham Lincoln in the film *Lincoln* earned him his third Academy Award. Day-Lewis also earned an Academy Award nomination for the film *Phantom Thread*.

AT A GLANCE

Notable Films: *My Beautiful Laundrette* (1985), *The Unbearable Lightness of Being* (1988), *My Left Foot* (1989), *The Last of the Mohicans* (1992), *In the Name of the Father* (1993), *The Boxer* (1997), *Gangs of New York* (2002), *There Will Be Blood* (2007), *Lincoln* (2012), *Phantom Thread* (2017)

Notable Awards: New York Film Critics Circle Awards, Best Supporting Actor (1986), Best Actor (1989, 2002, 2007, 2012); BAFTA Awards, Best Actor (1990, 2003, 2008, 2013); Academy Awards, Best Actor (1990, 2008, 2013); Screen Actors Guild Awards, Outstanding Performance by a Male Actor in a Leading Role (2003, 2008, 2013); Golden Globe Awards, Best Actor—Motion Picture, Drama (2008, 2013)

ROBERT DE NIRO

Robert De Niro had several minor film roles before appearing in *Bang the Drum Slowly*. In that movie, De Niro played a baseball player who had cancer. His performance caught the attention of critics and audiences. It kick-started his reputation as an excellent actor.

SUCCESS IN FILMS

De Niro appeared in *Mean Streets*, *Taxi Driver*, and *Raging Bull*. He received an Academy Award for Best Actor for *Raging Bull*. In that film, he played the real-life boxer Jake La Motta. De Niro gained more than 50 pounds (23 kg) for the role.

De Niro often played harsh, violent characters. One of his most famous roles was

As Robert De Niro got older, he took on more comedic roles playing grumpy old men.

as a mob boss in *The Godfather, Part II*. His performance earned him an Academy Award for Best Supporting Actor. Later in his career, De Niro landed roles in comedy films such as *Wag the Dog* and *Meet the Fockers*.

De Niro's acting as Vito Corleone, *left*, in *The Godfather Part II* made him a star.

AT A GLANCE

Notable Films: *Bang the Drum Slowly* (1973), *Mean Streets* (1973), *The Godfather, Part II* (1974), *Taxi Driver* (1976), *The Deer Hunter* (1978), *Raging Bull* (1980), *The King of Comedy* (1983), *Once upon a Time in America* (1984), *Goodfellas* (1990), *Heat* (1995), *The Irishman* (2019)

Notable Awards: Academy Awards, Best Supporting Actor (1975), Best Actor (1981); New York Film Critics Circle Awards, Best Supporting Actor (1974), Best Actor (1977, 1980, 1990); Los Angeles Film Critics Association Award, Best Actor (1980); National Board of Review, Best Actor (1980, 1990), Icon Award (2019); Golden Globe Awards, Best Actor—Motion Picture (1981), Cecil B. DeMille Award (2011); American Film Institute, Life Achievement Award (2003); Screen Actors Guild Award, Life Achievement Award (2020)

JUDI DENCH

Judi Dench was diagnosed with macular degeneration, which impacts her sight. In 2023, Dench said this disorder had made it impossible for her to learn lines and keep acting.

Judi Dench grew up in England. She studied drama in London. Dench appeared in many Shakespeare plays, including *Hamlet*, *Twelfth Night*, and *Macbeth*. Dench also was cast on television shows such as *A Fine Romance*.

POWERFUL ROLES

In many of her roles, Dench portrays a strong-willed, powerful woman. She acted as the boss for secret agent James Bond in several of the *Bond* movies. She also played British queens. She was Queen Victoria in *Mrs. Brown*. In *Shakespeare in Love*, she played Queen Elizabeth I and won an Academy Award for Best Supporting Actress. Dench gained more Academy Award nominations for her performances in the films *Iris*, *Notes on a Scandal*, *Chocolat*, and *Belfast*.

Dench has also advocated for various causes, such as protecting the environment. In 2019, she starred in *Judi Dench's Wild Borneo Adventure*. In this miniseries, Dench visited rainforests and coastlines and saw wildlife.

Dench received her Oscar at the 71st Academy Awards in 1999.

AT A GLANCE

Notable Films: *James Bond* series (1995, 1997, 1999, 2002, 2006, 2008, 2012, 2015), *Mrs. Brown* (1997), *Shakespeare in Love* (1998), *Chocolat* (2000), *Iris* (2001), *Mrs. Henderson Presents* (2005), *Notes on a Scandal* (2006), *The Best Exotic Marigold Hotel* (2012), *Philomena* (2013), *Victoria & Abdul* (2017)

Notable Awards: BAFTA Awards, Best Actress (1968, 1982, 2001), Best Actress in a Supporting Role (1987, 1989, 1999), Best Performance by an Actress in a Leading Role (1998, 2002), Academy Fellowship (2001); Golden Globe Awards, Best Actress—Motion Picture, Drama (1998), Best Actress—Limited Series, Anthology Series, or Television Motion Picture (2001); Academy Award, Best Supporting Actress (1999); Screen Actors Guild Award, Outstanding Performance by a Female Actor in a Supporting Role (2001)

JOHNNY DEPP

In 1984, Johnny Depp appeared in the horror film *A Nightmare on Elm Street*. That role launched Depp's acting career. Depp's fame grew with his role in *21 Jump Street*. In that television series, he played an undercover police officer.

UNCONVENTIONAL CHARACTERS

Over his career, Depp became known for portraying unconventional characters. For instance, in the movie *Edward Scissorhands*, Depp plays a man with scissors for hands. In *Charlie and the Chocolate Factory*, he stars as Willy Wonka, the quirky owner of a chocolate factory.

For his role in the film *Sweeney Todd: The Demon Barber of Fleet Street*, Depp received an Academy Award nomination and a Golden

Johnny Depp pursued a career in music when he was 16 years old, dropping out of high school to do so. He eventually turned to acting.

Depp played the iconic Captain Jack Sparrow in five of the *Pirates of the Caribbean* movies.

Globe Best Actor award. In 2003, Depp appeared in the first of the *Pirates of the Caribbean* movies. He received an Academy Award nomination for playing Captain Jack Sparrow.

AT A GLANCE

Notable Films: *Edward Scissorhands* (1990), *What's Eating Gilbert Grape* (1993), *Ed Wood* (1994), *Donnie Brasco* (1997), *Pirates of the Caribbean* series (2003, 2006, 2007, 2011, 2017), *Finding Neverland* (2004), *Charlie and the Chocolate Factory* (2005), *Sweeney Todd: The Demon Barber of Fleet Street* (2007), *Into the Woods* (2014), *Black Mass* (2015)

Notable Awards: Screen Actors Guild Award, Outstanding Performance by a Male Actor in a Leading Role (2004); Golden Globe Award, Best Actor—Motion Picture, Musical/Comedy (2008)

LEONARDO DiCAPRIO

Leonardo DiCaprio began acting in the children's television program *Romper Room* when he was five years old. In 1991, he had his first film role in the horror movie *Critters 3*. He received an Academy Award nomination for his role as a teen with a developmental disability in *What's Eating Gilbert Grape*.

A SMASHING SUCCESS

DiCaprio gained fame in the 1997 smash-hit movie *Titanic*. He played a

In addition to acting, Leonardo DiCaprio also produces films.

poor artist who falls in love with a rich woman as they travel on the ill-fated ship *Titanic*. The popular film was one of the highest-grossing movies ever. DiCaprio was also praised for his roles in *Revolutionary Road*, *Inception*, and *J. Edgar*. He has been nominated for an Academy Award six times. He won the Best Actor award for his performance in *The Revenant*.

AT A GLANCE

Notable Films: *What's Eating Gilbert Grape* (1993), *Titanic* (1997), *Catch Me If You Can* (2002), *The Aviator* (2004), *The Departed* (2006), *Django Unchained* (2012), *The Wolf of Wall Street* (2013), *The Revenant* (2015), *Once Upon a Time . . . in Hollywood* (2019), *Don't Look Up* (2021)

Notable Awards: National Board of Review, Best Supporting Actor (1993, 2012), Spotlight Award (2013); Golden Globe Awards, Best Actor—Motion Picture, Drama (2005, 2016), Best Actor—Motion Picture, Musical/Comedy (2014); Academy Award, Best Actor (2016); BAFTA Award, Best Leading Actor (2016); Screen Actors Guild Award, Outstanding Performance by a Male Actor in a Leading Role (2016)

In *The Revenant*, DiCaprio played a fur trapper seeking revenge for his son's death.

ROBERT DOWNEY JR.

After minor roles in films, in 1985 Robert Downey Jr. landed a spot on the television comedy show *Saturday Night Live*. Then he got attention from movie critics for his role as the actor Charlie Chaplin in the film *Chaplin*. Downey received a nomination for an Academy Award for this role.

HARDSHIPS AND REDEMPTION

Downey continued to have success in acting. But his substance abuse problems led to a three-year prison sentence in 1999. Downey was granted an early release from prison. In 2000, he got a role in the television show *Ally McBeal* and later received a Golden Globe Award. After more legal troubles related to his substance abuse, he

Robert Downey Jr. left high school to pursue an acting career.

Downney, *second from right*, attends a premiere for *The Avengers* in 2012.

AT A GLANCE

Notable Films: *Chaplin* (1992), *Short Cuts* (1993), *Natural Born Killers* (1994), *Wonder Boys* (2000), *Kiss Kiss Bang Bang* (2005), *Zodiac* (2007), *Tropic Thunder* (2008), *Iron Man* series (2008, 2010, 2013), *Sherlock Holmes* (2009), *Avengers* series (2012, 2015, 2018, 2019)

Notable Awards: BAFTA Award, Best Actor (1993); Golden Globe Awards, Best Supporting Actor—Television (2001), Best Actor—Motion Picture, Musical/Comedy (2010); Screen Actors Guild Award, Outstanding Performance by a Male Actor in a Comedy Series (2001)

relaunched his career in *Iron Man*. Downey continued playing the Iron Man role in the *Avengers* series.

ADAM DRIVER

Adam Driver developed an interest in acting while in high school. But he later joined the US Marines and served for almost three years. When he was discharged, Driver pursued his passion for acting.

BROADWAY, TELEVISION, AND FILM

Driver began performing on Broadway in 2010. He had minor television roles before his first film, *J. Edgar,* in 2011. Next, he landed a role in the television comedy *Girls*. He received three Emmy nominations for that role.

Driver played the villain Kylo Ren in *Star Wars: Episode VII—The Force Awakens*. He took on this role in two more *Star Wars* films in 2017 and 2019. In addition, film critics praised Driver for his

Adam Driver went to the Juilliard School. This is a prestigious performing arts school in New York.

Driver starred with Scarlett Johansson in *Marriage Story*, which focuses on a family going through a divorce.

roles in *Paterson* and *Silence*. He played a Jewish police detective who helps infiltrate the Ku Klux Klan in the film *BlacKkKlansman*. Driver received an Academy Award nomination for the role. In 2019, he received an Academy Award Best Actor nomination for his part in *Marriage Story*.

AT A GLANCE

Notable Films: *Hungry Hearts* (2014), *While We're Young* (2014), *Star Wars* series (2015, 2017, 2019), *Paterson* (2016), *Silence* (2016), *Logan Lucky* (2017), *BlacKkKlansman* (2018), *Marriage Story* (2019), *The Man Who Killed Don Quixote* (2018), *Annette* (2021)

Notable Awards: Los Angeles Film Critics Association Award, Best Actor (2016)

Clint Eastwood served in the US Army before moving to Hollywood to pursue acting. Eastwood's first big break was a role in the television Western *Rawhide*. His roles in films such as *A Fistful of Dollars* and *The Good, the Bad and the Ugly* built his fame as an actor.

MORE THAN AN ACTOR

Eastwood played police inspector Harry Callahan in the movie series *Dirty Harry*. This successful series has five films spanning almost two decades. In movies such as *Play Misty for Me*, *High Plains Drifter*,

Clint Eastwood often plays outsider characters who have a cold demeanor.

Notable Films: *A Fistful of Dollars* (1964), *The Good, the Bad and the Ugly* (1966), *Hang 'Em High* (1968), *Dirty Harry* (1971), *The Outlaw Josey Wales* (1976), *Unforgiven* (1992), *In the Line of Fire* (1993), *The Bridges of Madison County* (1995), *Million Dollar Baby* (2004)

Notable Awards: Golden Globe Awards, World Film Favorite (1971), Cecil B. DeMille Award (1988); Academy Awards, Best Picture (1993, 2005), Best Director (1993, 2005); American Film Institute, Life Achievement Award (1996); Cannes Film Festival, Golden Coach (2003), Special Award (2008), Honorary Golden Palm (2009)

The Outlaw Josey Wales, and *Unforgiven*, Eastwood acted and directed. His Western movie *Unforgiven* won an Academy Award for Best Picture. In addition, Eastwood directed *Million Dollar Baby*. This film also won Academy Award for Best Picture.

Eastwood played Rowdy Yates in *Rawhide*. The show ran from 1959 to 1965.

COLIN FARRELL

Colin Farrell has been nominated for three Golden Globe Awards and won two.

Colin Farrell was born in Ireland. After high school, he worked some odd jobs before attending acting school for about a year. Then he got a role in the television drama *Ballykissangel*. While working in Ireland, he had roles in several films and another television drama. In 2000, Farrell appeared in the US film *Tigerland*. He played the part of Roland Bozz, a soldier going through training before being shipped off to Vietnam. Film critics praised his acting.

AWARD NOMINATIONS AND WINS

In 2002, Farrell played a police officer in the science-fiction thriller *Minority Report*. He won a Best Actor Golden Globe Award for his role in the film *In Bruges*, an action comedy.

AT A GLANCE

Notable Films: *Tigerland* (2000), *Minority Report* (2002), *Phone Booth* (2003), *In Bruges* (2008), *Seven Psychopaths* (2012), *The Lobster* (2016), *The Killing of a Sacred Deer* (2017), *Widows* (2018), *After Yang* (2021), *The Banshees of Inisherin* (2022)

Notable Awards: Golden Globe Awards, Best Actor—Motion Picture, Musical/Comedy (2009, 2023); National Board of Review, Best Actor (2022); New York Film Critics Circle Award, Best Actor (2022)

In 2022, he starred in the dark comedy *The Banshees of Inisherin*. Farrell received an Academy Award nomination and a Golden Globe Award for his role in the film.

Farrell poses with *The Banshees of Inisherin* director Martin McDonagh at the 2023 Golden Globe Awards.

HARRISON FORD

After college, Harrison Ford started looking for acting work. He got minor roles. His role in the popular 1973 film *American Graffiti* gave his acting career the boost it needed.

A SPACE PILOT AND AN ADVENTURER

Ford's true fame came with his portrayal of pilot Han Solo in the wildly popular *Star Wars* series. He acted in *A New Hope*,

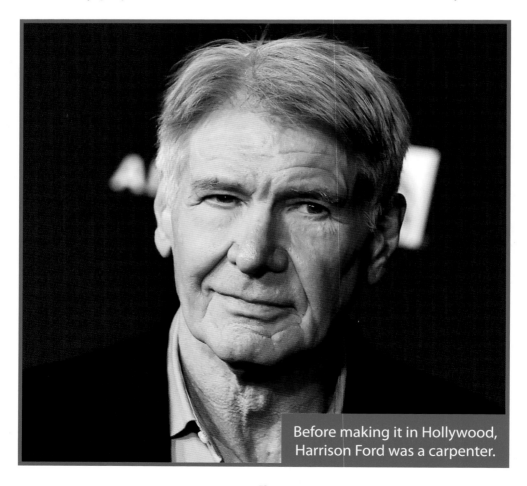

Before making it in Hollywood, Harrison Ford was a carpenter.

Ford starred alongside Mark Hamill, *left*, and Carrie Fisher, *center*, in the *Star Wars* series.

The Empire Strikes Back, *Return of the Jedi*, and *The Force Awakens*. Ford also played an adventurous archaeologist named Indiana Jones in the popular *Indiana Jones* series.

Ford received an Academy Award nomination for his performance in *Witness*. In that film, he played a city detective hiding in an Amish community. The American Film Institute honored Ford with a Life Achievement Award in 2000.

AT A GLANCE

Notable Films: *American Graffiti* (1973), *Star Wars* series (1977, 1980, 1983, 2015), *Indiana Jones* series (1981, 1984, 1989, 2008, 2023), *Blade Runner* (1982), *Witness* (1985), *The Mosquito Coast* (1986), *Jack Ryan* series (1992, 1994), *The Fugitive* (1993), *42* (2013)

Notable Awards: American Film Institute, Life Achievement Award (2000); Golden Globe Award, Cecil B. DeMille Award (2002)

JODIE FOSTER

Jodie Foster started acting in commercials at age two. By age six, she had her first role in the television show *Mayberry R.F.D.* Even while acting, Foster was an excellent student. She was valedictorian of her high school class. She studied at the prestigious Yale University. While still a teen, Foster received critics' praise for her role in *Taxi Driver*. She won Academy Awards for Best Actress in the films *The Accused* and *The Silence of the Lambs*. In addition to acting, Foster also directed several films and television shows.

Jodie Foster's first time directing was for the 1991 film *Little Man Tate*.

AT A GLANCE

Notable Films: *Alice Doesn't Live Here Anymore* (1974), *Taxi Driver* (1976), *Freaky Friday* (1976), *Bugsy Malone* (1976), *The Little Girl Who Lives Down the Lane* (1976), *The Accused* (1988), *The Silence of the Lambs* (1991), *Contact* (1997), *Panic Room* (2002), *The Brave One* (2007)

Notable Awards: National Board of Review, Best Actress (1988); Golden Globe Awards, Best Actress—Motion Picture, Drama (1989, 1992), Cecil B. DeMille Award (2013), Best Supporting Actress—Motion Picture (2021); Academy Awards, Best Actress (1989, 1992); Cannes Film Festival, Honorary Golden Palm (2021)

JAMIE FOXX

Jamie Foxx studied music in high school and college. While in college, he started performing in comedy clubs. Audiences loved his funny impersonations. The comedy club performances helped him land a role on the hit television show *In Living Color*. Soon Foxx's television success brought him movie roles. He earned a Best Actor Academy Award for playing the singer Ray Charles in the movie *Ray*. Some of his other significant films include *Django Unchained*, *The Amazing Spider-Man 2*, and *Annie*.

AT A GLANCE

Notable Films: *The Truth about Cats & Dogs* (1996), *Ali* (2001), *Ray* (2004), *Collateral* (2004), *Dreamgirls* (2006), *Horrible Bosses* (2011), *Django Unchained* (2012), *The Amazing Spider-Man 2* (2014), *Baby Driver* (2017), *Just Mercy* (2019)

Notable Awards: Screen Actors Guild Award, Outstanding Performance by a Male Actor in a Leading Role (2005); National Board of Review, Best Actor (2004); Academy Award, Best Actor (2005); BAFTA Award, Best Performance by an Actor in a Leading Role (2005); Golden Globe Award, Best Actor—Musical/Comedy (2005)

Jamie Foxx is an actor, musician, and comedian.

Morgan Freeman served in the US Air Force before turning his focus to acting. His first Broadway role was in an all-Black production of *Hello Dolly!* in 1967. During the 1970s and early 1980s, Freeman acted in several television roles.

AN ESTABLISHED CAREER

Freeman received his first Academy Award nomination for his role in *Street Smart*. He played a dangerous criminal in the film. Freeman also received an Academy Award nomination for Best Actor for *Driving Miss Daisy*. He played a Civil War (1861–1865) soldier in *Glory* and a gunslinger in the Western *Unforgiven*. Freeman got another Academy Award nomination for his role as a convict in *The Shawshank Redemption*. He won the Academy

Morgan Freeman is known for bringing humor and depth to his characters.

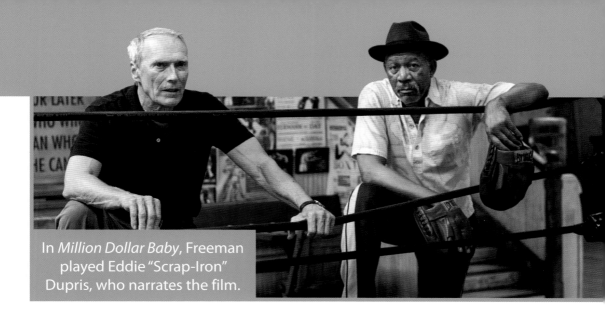

In *Million Dollar Baby*, Freeman played Eddie "Scrap-Iron" Dupris, who narrates the film.

Award for Best Supporting Actor for playing a boxer in *Million Dollar Baby*. Freeman also took on the role of Lucius Fox, a research-and-development expert, in *The Dark Knight* trilogy. Freeman is known for his deep, calm, and distinctive voice.

AT A GLANCE

Notable Films: *Street Smart* (1987), *Glory* (1989), *Driving Miss Daisy* (1989), *Unforgiven* (1992), *The Shawshank Redemption* (1994), *Amistad* (1997), *Nurse Betty* (2000), *Million Dollar Baby* (2004), *The Dark Knight* trilogy (2005, 2008, 2012), *Invictus* (2009)

Notable Awards: New York Film Critics Circle Award, Best Supporting Actor (1987); National Board of Review, Best Actor (1989), Career Achievement Award (2003), Best Actor (2009); Golden Globe Awards, Best Actor—Motion Picture, Musical/Comedy (1990), Cecil B. DeMille Award (2012); Academy Award, Best Supporting Actor (2005); Screen Actors Guild Awards, Outstanding Performance by a Male Actor in a Supporting Role (2005), Life Achievement Award (2018); American Film Institute, Life Achievement Award (2011)

CLARK GABLE

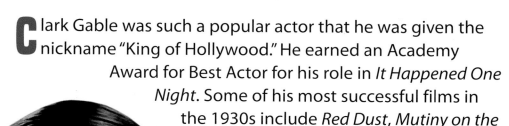

Clark Gable was such a popular actor that he was given the nickname "King of Hollywood." He earned an Academy Award for Best Actor for his role in *It Happened One Night*. Some of his most successful films in the 1930s include *Red Dust*, *Mutiny on the Bounty*, and *Gone with the Wind*. At first, Gable turned down the offer to play Rhett Butler in *Gone with the Wind*. But he then reconsidered and took the part. The nearly four-hour movie, set during the US Civil War, is one of the most popular films ever made. However, people have criticized the movie's portrayal of Black people, who were cast in

In *Gone with the Wind*, Clark Gable's character was in love with the film's protagonist, Scarlett O'Hara.

Gable joined the war effort in 1942.

stereotypical and demeaning roles.

JOINING THE WAR

Gable stepped away from acting during World War II. He served with the Army Air Corps. Gable returned to acting in 1945 as the war ended. Critics regard his last film, *The Misfits*, as one of his best performances.

When Judy Garland was two years old, she sang onstage at her local movie theater. In 1935, when Garland was a young teen, the largest motion-picture studio, Metro-Goldwyn-Mayer, signed her to an acting contract. Garland appeared in her first film, *Every Sunday,* a year later.

THE WIZARD OF OZ

One of Garland's best-known roles was playing Dorothy in *The Wizard of Oz*. In that movie,

In *The Wizard of Oz*, scenes in Kansas are in black and white. Scenes in the magical realm are in color.

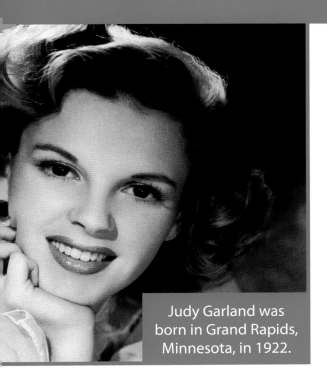

Judy Garland was born in Grand Rapids, Minnesota, in 1922.

AT A GLANCE

Notable Films: *The Wizard of Oz* (1939), *For Me and My Gal* (1942), *Meet Me in St. Louis* (1944), *The Harvey Girls* (1946), *Easter Parade* (1948), *In the Good Old Summertime* (1949), *A Star Is Born* (1954), *Judgment at Nuremberg* (1961), *I Could Go On Singing* (1963), *A Child Is Waiting* (1963)

Notable Awards: Academy Award, Outstanding Performance as a Screen Juvenile (1940); Golden Globe Awards, Best Actress—Musical/Comedy (1955), Cecil B. DeMille Award (1962); Grammy Award, Lifetime Achievement Award (1997)

Garland's character is transported from rural Kansas to a magical realm. Garland put her voice to work in the film. She sang the popular song "Over the Rainbow." Garland won a special Academy Award for her role in the movie.

Another noteworthy film of Garland's was *Meet Me in St. Louis*. In that film, she played Esther Smith, a daughter in a family that is planning to relocate to New York City. *The Harvey Girls* and *Easter Parade* are among Garland's other well-known 1940s films.

TOM HANKS

Tom Hanks studied drama in college. Then he moved to New York City. Hanks's early television and film roles were comedy parts. *Splash* and *The Money Pit* were two of his early comedy films.

AN AWARD-WINNING ACTOR

Hanks received an Academy Award nomination for his role as a boy in an adult body in *Big*. Hanks also starred with actor Meg Ryan in three romantic comedies: *Joe versus the Volcano*, *Sleepless in Seattle*, and *You've Got Mail*. He won back-to-back Academy Awards for Best Actor for *Philadelphia* in 1994 and *Forrest Gump* in 1995. His roles in *Saving Private Ryan* and

In addition to television and movie roles, Tom Hanks has also starred on Broadway. He appeared in his first Broadway play in 2013.

Cast Away earned him two more Academy Award nominations. Hanks received another Academy Award nomination for playing Mister Rogers in the film *A Beautiful Day in the Neighborhood*. In addition to acting, Hanks has written and directed films.

Hanks, *right*, played Captain Miller in *Saving Private Ryan*.

AT A GLANCE

Notable Films: *Big* (1988), *A League of Their Own* (1992), *Sleepless in Seattle* (1993), *Philadelphia* (1993), *Forrest Gump* (1994), *Apollo 13* (1995), *Toy Story* series (1995, 1999, 2010, 2019), *Saving Private Ryan* (1998), *Catch Me If You Can* (2002), *A Beautiful Day in the Neighborhood* (2019)

Notable Awards: Golden Globe Awards, Best Actor—Motion Picture, Musical/Comedy (1989), Best Actor—Motion Picture, Drama (1994, 1995, 2001), Cecil B. DeMille Award (2020); Academy Awards, Best Actor (1994, 1995); National Board of Review, Best Actor (1994, 2017); New York Film Critics Circle Award, Best Actor (2000); American Film Institute, Life Achievement Award (2002)

ANNE HATHAWAY

A nne Hathaway's mother was a stage actress. Traveling for her mother's work inspired Hathaway to be an actress too. Hathaway's early acting roles included popular family-friendly films like *The Princess Diaries* and *Ella Enchanted*. Over time, she took on more adult roles in successful films like *Nicholas Nickleby*, *Brokeback Mountain*, and *The Devil Wears Prada*.

Anne Hathaway has used her position in the public eye to raise awareness for social causes such as gender equality.

PLAYING DIFFERENT CHARACTERS

In 2007, Hathaway played the role of the author Jane Austen in *Becoming Jane*. The next year, she appeared in the film *Rachel Getting Married*, which was praised by critics and brought Hathaway several award nominations. She played Catwoman in *The Dark Knight Rises*. She also starred in *Les Misérables*, playing the character Fantine—a French woman who gets pregnant and lives in poverty. Hathaway won the Best Supporting Actress Academy Award for the role. Critics praised Hathaway for her part in the film *Ocean's 8*, where she played the self-absorbed actor Daphne Kluger.

AT A GLANCE

Notable Films: *The Princess Diaries* (2001), *Nicholas Nickleby* (2002), *Brokeback Mountain* (2005), *The Devil Wears Prada* (2006), *Rachel Getting Married* (2008), *Love and Other Drugs* (2010), *Les Misérables* (2012), *The Dark Knight Rises* (2012), *Interstellar* (2014), *Colossal* (2016)

Notable Awards: National Board of Review, Best Actress (2008); Emmy Award, Outstanding Voice-Over Performance (2010); Academy Award, Best Supporting Actress (2013); BAFTA Award, Best Supporting Actress (2013); Golden Globe Award, Best Supporting Actress—Motion Picture (2013); Screen Actors Guild Award, Outstanding Performance by a Female Actor in a Supporting Role (2013)

Hathaway, *bottom left*, and the rest of the *Les Misérables* cast performed at the 2013 Academy Awards.

SALMA HAYEK

Salma Hayek was born in Mexico. She decided to be an actress after seeing *Willy Wonka & the Chocolate Factory*. Her first acting role was in a Mexican daytime television drama. Hayek then moved to Los Angeles to pursue acting. Her small role in *Mi Vida Loca* brought her attention. Hayek's next role was in *Desperado*. With her appearance in this film, Hayek's fame soared with fans and film critics.

Salma Hayek has opened doors for many other Latina actors who want to pursue careers in the United States.

DIRECTOR AND PRODUCER

Creating a movie requires a team of people doing many different jobs. The actors are just one piece in the movie-making process. A movie must also have a director and a producer. The director supervises the creative part of making the movie. The producer supervises the business side. There is usually just one director for a movie, but there might be several producers.

ACTING, DIRECTING, AND PRODUCING

Hayek was nominated for an Academy Award for her role in the film *Frida*. She produced and starred in the film, which told the story of the Mexican painter Frida Kahlo. The film received six Academy Award nominations, including the Best Actress nomination for Hayek. During her career, she has worked as an actor, director, and producer.

Hayek received the Anthony Quinn Award in 2009. This award is given to people who have made contributions to the arts.

AT A GLANCE

Notable Films: *Mi Vida Loca* (1993), *Desperado* (1995), *Timecode* (2000), *Traffic* (2000), *Frida* (2002), *Puss in Boots* (2011), *Muppets Most Wanted* (2014), *Tale of Tales* (2015), *Sausage Party* (2016), *Beatriz at Dinner* (2017), *Puss in Boots: The Last Wish* (2022)

Notable Awards: Cannes Film Festival, Kering Women in Motion Award (2021); American Latino Media Arts Awards, Outstanding Actor/Actress in a Made for Television Movie or Miniseries (2002), Anthony Quinn Award for Industry Excellence (2009)

AUDREY HEPBURN

Audrey Hepburn was born on May 4, 1929, in Belgium. In her early twenties, she began acting, modeling, and dancing. Critics praised Hepburn for her role in the Broadway play *Gigi* in 1951. Her first American film was *Roman Holiday*. She played the role of a young princess. Hepburn won the Academy Award for Best Actress.

SOPHISTICATED ROLES

Hepburn often played sophisticated women. In her films such as *Breakfast at Tiffany's*, *Charade*, and *Two for the Road*, she portrayed stylish, worldly characters. After her role in the thriller film *Wait Until Dark*, she stopped acting to focus on her marriage and

Audrey Hepburn grew up in Europe during World War II, where her family faced wartime hardships.

family. She returned to acting in the 1976 film *Robin and Marian*. Hepburn died in 1993. The Academy of Motion Picture Arts and Sciences honored Hepburn with the Jean Hersholt Humanitarian Award after her death.

AT A GLANCE

Notable Films: *Roman Holiday* (1953), *Sabrina* (1954), *Funny Face* (1957), *The Nun's Story* (1959), *Breakfast at Tiffany's* (1961), *Charade* (1963), *My Fair Lady* (1964), *How to Steal a Million* (1966), *Two for the Road* (1967), *Wait Until Dark* (1967)

Notable Awards: Academy Awards, Best Actress (1954), Jean Hersholt Humanitarian Award (1993); Golden Globe Awards, Best Actress— Drama (1954), Henrietta Award (1955), Cecil B. DeMille Award (1990); Screen Actors Guild Award, Life Achievement Award (1993); Grammy Award, Best Spoken Word Album for Children (1994)

Roman Holiday is a romantic comedy. In the movie, Hepburn plays Princess Ann.

KATHARINE HEPBURN

After college, Katharine Hepburn acted in some Broadway plays. She moved on to Hollywood film roles in the 1930s. Hepburn's third film, *Morning Glory*, brought her an Academy Award for Best Actress. She starred in several Broadway plays and movies that were not so successful. However, her acting in the comedy film *The Philadelphia Story* was a hit with critics and fans. Her role in *The African Queen* continued to increase her popularity. She also won Academy Awards for *Guess Who's Coming to Dinner*, *The Lion in Winter*, and *On Golden Pond*.

A LONG CAREER

Hepburn was a strong, determined woman, much like the roles she played in films. She often wore slacks long before it was

Katharine Hepburn was born on May 12, 1907, in Hartford, Connecticut.

In *The Philadelphia Story*, Hepburn's character is about to get remarried when her ex-husband shows up and complicates things.

widely acceptable or fashionable for women to dress that way. Hepburn's career covered more than six decades. She won three of her four Academy Awards after age 60.

AT A GLANCE

Notable Films: *Morning Glory* (1933), *Bringing Up Baby* (1938), *The Philadelphia Story* (1940), *The African Queen* (1951), *Summertime* (1955), *Suddenly, Last Summer* (1959), *Long Day's Journey into Night* (1962), *Guess Who's Coming to Dinner* (1967), *The Lion in Winter* (1968), *On Golden Pond* (1981)

Notable Awards: Academy Awards, Best Actress (1934, 1968, 1969, 1982); New York Film Critics Circle Award, Best Actress (1940); Cannes Film Festival, Best Actress (1962); BAFTA Awards, Best Actress (1969, 1983); Emmy Award, Outstanding Lead Actress in a Special Program—Drama/Comedy (1975); Screen Actors Guild Award, Life Achievement Award (1980)

CHARLTON HESTON

Charlton Heston was born on October 4, 1923, in Wilmette, Illinois. He studied acting in college. Then he moved to New York City. His Broadway debut role was in Shakespeare's *Antony and Cleopatra*. He also began to land jobs in television and film. Heston is known for playing historical and biblical characters. He won

In his role as Moses, Charlton Heston holds God's Ten Commandments.

the Academy Award for Best Actor in the film *Ben-Hur*, where he played a Jewish prince named Judah Ben-Hur. Heston is best known for his role as Moses in *The Ten Commandments*.

AT A GLANCE

Notable Films: *The Greatest Show on Earth* (1952), *The Ten Commandments* (1956), *Touch of Evil* (1958), *Ben-Hur* (1959), *El Cid* (1961), *Planet of the Apes* (1968), *Will Penny* (1967), *Julius Caesar* (1970), *Soylent Green* (1973), *Earthquake* (1974)

Notable Awards: Academy Awards, Best Actor (1960), Jean Hersholt Humanitarian Award (1978); Golden Globe Award, Cecil B. DeMille Award (1967); Screen Actors Guild Award, Life Achievement Award (1972)

DUSTIN HOFFMAN

Dustin Hoffman attended college in California to study music but then moved to New York City to pursue acting. Hoffman often plays antiheroes. These are main characters who don't have typical hero qualities. Hoffman is known for tackling challenging roles. For example, in *Tootsie* he played a male actor pretending to be female. In *Rain Man*, he portrayed a middle-aged man with autism. Hoffman won Academy Awards for Best Actor for the films *Kramer vs. Kramer* and *Rain Man*.

Dustin Hoffman received the Cecil B. DeMille Award in 1997.

AT A GLANCE

Notable Films: *The Graduate* (1967), *Midnight Cowboy* (1969), *Little Big Man* (1970), *Straw Dogs* (1971), *Lenny* (1974), *All the President's Men* (1976), *Kramer vs. Kramer* (1979), *Tootsie* (1982), *Rain Man* (1988), *Wag the Dog* (1997)

Notable Awards: Golden Globe Awards, Best Actor—Motion Picture, Drama (1980, 1989), Best Actor—Motion Picture, Musical/Comedy (1983), Best Actor—Limited Series, Anthology Series, or Television Motion Picture (1986), Cecil B. DeMille Award (1997); New York Film Critics Circle Award, Best Actor (1979); Academy Awards, Best Actor (1980, 1989); Emmy Award, Outstanding Lead Actor in a Miniseries or a Special (1986); American Film Institute, Life Achievement Award (1999)

PHILIP SEYMOUR HOFFMAN

Philip Seymour Hoffman's first acting work was in theaters in New York City and Chicago, Illinois. Hoffman soon landed some movie roles. His part in *Boogie Nights* propelled him to fame. In that movie, Hoffman played an awkward secondary character named Scotty.

A WIDE RANGE OF FILMS

Hoffman showcased his strong acting skills in a range of film genres including comedies, serious dramas, and action thrillers. Film critics and fans recognized him as a strong actor on the stage and in movies. Hoffman received Academy

Philip Seymour Hoffman has been in action movies such as *Mission: Impossible III*, where he starred as the villain.

Hoffman appeared in the Broadway play *Death of a Salesman* in 2012.

Award nominations for Best Actor four times. He won the Best Actor award for his role as the author Truman Capote in the film *Capote*. He was also praised for his roles in the films *Charlie Wilson's War*, *Doubt,* and *The Master*. While starring in movies, Hoffman also continued acting in the theater.

AT A GLANCE

Notable Films: *Boogie Nights* (1997), *The Talented Mr. Ripley* (1999), *Punch-Drunk Love* (2002), *Capote* (2005), *Before the Devil Knows You're Dead* (2007), *Doubt* (2008), *Synecdoche, New York* (2008), *The Ides of March* (2011), *Moneyball* (2011), *Hunger Games* series (2013, 2014, 2015)

Notable Awards: National Board of Review, Best Supporting Actor (1999), Best Actor (2005); Los Angeles Film Critics Association Award, Best Actor (2005); Screen Actors Guild Award, Outstanding Performance by a Male Actor in a Leading Role (2005); Academy Award, Best Actor (2006); BAFTA Award, Best Performance by an Actor in a Leading Role (2006); Golden Globe Award, Best Actor—Motion Picture, Drama (2006)

ANTHONY HOPKINS

Anthony Hopkins's first stage role was in *Julius Caesar* in 1964. Hopkins had success in several other plays too. Then he landed the role of Prince Richard the Lionheart in *The Lion in Winter*. Hopkins won Emmy Awards for his parts in *The Lindbergh Kidnapping Case* and *The Bunker*, which were television films. For his role as the cannibal Dr. Hannibal Lecter in *The Silence of the Lambs*, he won a Best Actor Academy Award.

Anthony Hopkins was born in Wales.

A VETERAN IN THE BUSINESS

Following his success in *The Silence of the Lambs*, Hopkins acted in *Dracula*, *Legends of the Fall*, and *Nixon*. He earned another Academy Award nomination for his role in *The Two Popes*. In 2021, at age 83, Hopkins became the oldest actor to win an Academy Award for Best Actor. He won for his performance in *The Father*. In that movie, he played a man dealing with dementia.

Hopkins and his costar Jodie Foster both won Academy Awards for *The Silence of the Lambs*.

AT A GLANCE

Notable Films: *The Lion in Winter* (1968), *The Elephant Man* (1980), *The Silence of the Lambs* (1991), *Howards End* (1992), *The Remains of the Day* (1993), *Shadowlands* (1993), *Nixon* (1995), *Amistad* (1997), *The Two Popes* (2019), *The Father* (2020)

Notable Awards: BAFTA Awards, Best Actor (1973, 1992, 1994, 2021), Academy Fellowship (2008); Emmy Awards, Outstanding Lead Actor in a Drama or Comedy Special (1976), Outstanding Lead Actor in a Limited Series or a Special (1981); Academy Awards, Best Actor (1992, 2021); Los Angeles Film Critics Association Award, Best Actor (1993); Golden Globe Award, Cecil B. DeMille Award (2006)

Samuel L. Jackson was active in the civil rights movement in the 1960s. He also worked as a social worker. In college, Jackson focused on acting. After graduating, he performed political skits with the Black Image Theatre Company.

SKYROCKETING TO FAME

Jackson's early films included *Do the Right Thing* and *Jungle Fever*. With his role as a hit man in *Pulp Fiction*, Jackson's fame rose. He earned an Academy Award nomination for his performance in that film. Some of his other roles in the 1990s included *Die Hard with a Vengeance* and *A Time to Kill*.

Samuel L. Jackson has featured in many action movies.

Jackson starred with Chris Evans, *left*, and Tom Hiddleston, *right*, in the *Avengers* series.

He also acted in some of the *Star Wars* movies, where he played a Jedi named Mace Windu. In 2009, Jackson signed a contract with Marvel Comics to make nine superhero movies playing the character Nick Fury. These included films like *Iron Man 2* and *The Avengers*. In 2022, Jackson received an honorary Academy Award for lifetime achievement.

AT A GLANCE

Notable Films: *Do the Right Thing* (1989), *Jungle Fever* (1991), *Pulp Fiction* (1994), *Jackie Brown* (1997), *A Time to Kill* (1996), *Star Wars* series (1999, 2002, 2005), *Unbreakable* (2000), *Django Unchained* (2012), *The Hateful Eight* (2015)

Notable Awards: Cannes Film Festival, Best Supporting Actor (1991); New York Film Critics Circle Award, Best Supporting Actor (1991); Academy Award, Honorary Award (2022); BAFTA Award, Best Actor in a Supporting Role (1995)

SCARLETT JOHANSSON

Scarlett Johansson was interested in acting as a child. At age eight, she had a role in the off-Broadway play *Sophistry*. At age nine, she had her first film role in *North*. Critics praised her acting in the films *The Horse Whisperer* in 1998 and *Ghost World* in 2001.

VARIED ROLES

Johansson has featured in historical

Scarlett Johansson has a twin brother and three other siblings.

films such as *Girl with a Pearl Earring* and *The Other Boleyn Girl*. She has also been in modern films like *Ghost World* and *Lost in Translation*. In 2010, she first played Natasha Romanoff, also

BROADWAY VS. OFF-BROADWAY

Broadway is the name of a long street in New York City. Part of Broadway runs through an area where many theaters are located. Broadway plays are those held in the theaters that have 500 or more seats. Off-Broadway plays are held in theaters with between 99 and 499 seats.

called the Black Widow, in *Iron Man 2*. She played this role in several other films as well. Two of Johansson's 2019 films, *Marriage Story* and *Jojo Rabbit*, earned her Academy Award nominations. Besides her movie roles, Johansson has acted in several Broadway plays, including *A View from the Bridge*, which won her a Tony Award for Best Actress.

AT A GLANCE

Notable Films: *Manny & Lo* (1996), *The Horse Whisperer* (1998), *Ghost World* (2001), *Lost in Translation* (2003), *Girl with a Pearl Earring* (2003), *Match Point* (2005), *Under the Skin* (2013), *Hail, Caesar!* (2016), *Marriage Story* (2019), *Jojo Rabbit* (2019), *Black Widow* (2021)

Notable Awards: BAFTA Award, Best Performance by an Actress in a Leading Role (2004); Los Angeles Film Critics Association Award, New Generation Award (2004); Tony Award, Best Actress (2010)

Johansson appeared in the animated movies *Sing* and *Sing 2*, where she showed off her singing voice.

JAMES EARL JONES

James Earl Jones studied drama in college. He later served in the US Army. Then he moved to New York City to act. Jones won a Tony Award for his role as a boxer in the play *The Great White Hope*. He played the same role in the film version and received an Academy Award nomination. Jones received another Tony Award for his role in *Fences*. This Broadway play focused on race relations and Black life in the 1950s.

A BOOMING VOICE

Jones's first film role was in the 1964 movie *Dr. Strangelove*.

VOICE ACTING

When an actor performs only a speaking part in a film, it is known as voice acting or a voice-over. This happens in animated television shows, movies, video games, and audiobooks. James Earl Jones is just one of many actors who lends his voice to animated film roles. Some other famous movie actors who also do this work are Morgan Freeman, Tom Hanks, Kristen Bell, and Mila Kunis.

In 2015, James Earl Jones, *second from left*, appeared in Broadway's *The Gin Game*.

His other popular movies include *Matewan*, *Field of Dreams*, and the *Jack Ryan* films. With his booming, deep voice, Jones is well known for being the voice of Darth Vader in the *Star Wars* movies. He also was the voice actor for Mufasa in *The Lion King* in 1994. Jones received a Tony Award for lifetime achievement in 2017. He got an honorary Academy Award in 2011.

Jones spent more than 70 years acting.

AT A GLANCE

Notable Films: *Dr. Strangelove* (1964), *The Great White Hope* (1970), *Star Wars* series (1977, 1980, 1983, 2016, 2019), *Conan the Barbarian* (1982), *Coming to America* (1988), *Matewan* (1987), *Jack Ryan* series (1990, 1992, 1994), *The Lion King* (1994), *Cry, the Beloved Country* (1995), *A Family Thing* (1996)

Notable Awards: Tony Awards, Best Actor (1969, 1987); Grammy Award, Best Spoken Word Recording (1977); Emmy Awards, Outstanding Lead Actor in a Drama Series (1991), Outstanding Supporting Actor in a Miniseries or a Special (1991); National Board of Review, Career Achievement Award (1995); Screen Actors Guild Award, Life Achievement Award (2009); Academy Award, Honorary Award (2012)

Starting out, Michael B. Jordan pursued modeling and then acting. He played the role of a teen drug dealer in the television series *The Wire* and a high school quarterback in *Friday Night Lights*. Jordan also played a recovering alcoholic in the television series *Parenthood*. In 2012, he had a role in the war film *Red Tails*, a story about the Tuskegee Airmen. These Black airmen served in the US Army during World War II.

PLAYING A VILLAIN AND AN ACTIVIST

Jordan was praised for his role as Oscar Grant in *Fruitvale Station*. This film told the story of Grant, who was shot by police in California. Jordan also played the part of Adonis Creed in the

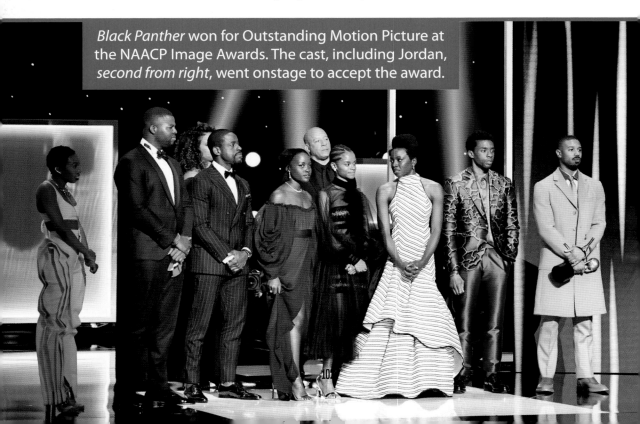

Black Panther won for Outstanding Motion Picture at the NAACP Image Awards. The cast, including Jordan, *second from right*, went onstage to accept the award.

boxing films *Creed* and *Creed II*. In *Black Panther*, Jordan played the villain Erik Killmonger. With the 2019 film *Just Mercy*, Jordan stepped into the role of activist and lawyer Bryan Stevenson. In 2023, *Creed III* was released. Jordan was the director.

Michael B. Jordan was a teenager when he first appeared on television.

AT A GLANCE

Notable Films: *Hardball* (2001), *Red Tails* (2012), *Fruitvale Station* (2013), *That Awkward Moment* (2014), *Fantastic Four* (2015), *Creed* (2015), *Creed II* (2018), *Black Panther* (2018), *Just Mercy* (2019), *A Journal for Jordan* (2021), *Without Remorse* (2021)
Notable Awards: National Board of Review, Breakthrough Performance by an Actor (2013)

GRACE KELLY

Grace Kelly was born on November 12, 1929, in Philadelphia, Pennsylvania. She is best known for being an American actress who became a European princess. Her acting career lasted just five years. It ended when Kelly left acting to marry Prince Rainier III of Monaco in 1956.

Kelly made her debut in a Broadway play in 1949. She appeared in her first film, *Fourteen Hours,* when she was 22. Kelly earned an Academy Award for Best Actress in *The Country Girl*.

AT A GLANCE

Notable Films: *Fourteen Hours* (1951), *High Noon* (1952), *Mogambo* (1953), *Rear Window* (1954), *The Country Girl* (1954), *To Catch a Thief* (1955), *Dial M for Murder* (1954), *The Bridges at Toko-Ri* (1954), *High Society* (1956), *The Swan* (1956)

Notable Awards: National Board of Review, Best Actress (1954); New York Film Critics Circle Award, Best Actress (1954); Golden Globe Awards, Best Supporting Actress (1954), Best Actress— Drama (1955), World Film Favorite (1956); Academy Award, Best Actress (1955)

Grace Kelly appeared in 11 movies before retiring.

104

NICOLE KIDMAN

Nicole Kidman is married to country music star Keith Urban.

Nicole Kidman grew up in Australia. She began acting in television films as a teen. She had roles in several successful 1990s films including *Days of Thunder*, *Billy Bathgate*, and *To Die For*. She received her first Academy Award nomination for her role in the musical *Moulin Rouge!* Kidman won the Academy Award for Best Actress for her portrayal of author Virginia Woolf in *The Hours*. She received three more Academy Award nominations for *Rabbit Hole*, *Lion*, and *Being the Ricardos*.

AT A GLANCE

Notable Films: *To Die For* (1995), *Eyes Wide Shut* (1999), *Moulin Rouge!* (2001), *The Others* (2001), *The Hours* (2002), *Cold Mountain* (2003), *Rabbit Hole* (2010), *Boy Erased* (2018), *Bombshell* (2019), *Being the Ricardos* (2021)

Notable Awards: Golden Globe Awards, Best Actress—Motion Picture, Musical/Comedy (1996, 2002), Best Actress—Motion Picture, Drama (2003, 2022); BAFTA Award, Best Performance by an Actress in a Leading Role (2003); Academy Award, Best Actress (2003); Emmy Awards, Outstanding Limited Series (2017), Outstanding Lead Actress in a Limited Series or Movie (2017); American Film Institute, Life Achievement Award (2023)

Jennifer Lawrence received an Academy Award nomination for Best Actress for *Winter's Bone*, in which she played Ree Dolly, a girl who searches for her missing father. Lawrence also played the role of shape-shifting Mystique in *X-Men: First Class*. She played the character again in three more *X-Men* films.

SOARING FAME

Lawrence gained more fame when she starred as Katniss Everdeen in *The Hunger Games* and its sequels. The movies were based on the best-selling dystopian novels by Suzanne Collins. At age 22, Lawrence

Jennifer Lawrence is known for giving honest and up-front opinions.

won an Academy Award for Best Actress for her role in *Silver Linings Playbook*. She received another Academy Award nomination for her portrayal as the wife of a con artist in *American Hustle*. In the movie *Causeway*, Lawrence starred as a war veteran who comes home with a brain injury.

Lawrence won Best Actress at the 85th Academy Awards.

AT A GLANCE

Notable Films: *Winter's Bone* (2010), *X-Men* series (2011, 2014, 2016, 2019), *Silver Linings Playbook* (2012), *Hunger Games* series (2012, 2013, 2014, 2015), *American Hustle* (2013), *Joy* (2015), *Passengers* (2016), *Mother!* (2017), *Red Sparrow* (2018), *Causeway* (2022)

Notable Awards: Academy Award, Best Actress (2013); New York Film Critics Circle Award, Best Supporting Actress (2013); Screen Actors Guild Award, Outstanding Performance by a Female Actor in a Leading Role (2013); Golden Globe Awards, Best Actress—Motion Picture, Musical/Comedy (2013, 2016), Best Supporting Actress—Motion Picture (2014); BAFTA Award, Best Supporting Actress (2014)

HEATH LEDGER

Heath Ledger grew up in Australia and acted in plays while in junior high.

Heath Ledger appeared on Australian television shows such as *Home and Away*. His first Hollywood film was the romantic comedy *10 Things I Hate about You*. He played a handsome high school student who tried to win over his classmate's heart. The film threw Ledger into the spotlight.

AT A GLANCE

Notable Films: *10 Things I Hate about You* (1999), *The Patriot* (2000), *Monster's Ball* (2001), *Lords of Dogtown* (2005), *Casanova* (2005), *Brokeback Mountain* (2005), *Candy* (2006), *I'm Not There* (2007), *The Dark Knight* (2008), *The Imaginarium of Doctor Parnassus* (2009)

Notable Awards: New York Film Critics Circle Award, Best Actor (2005); Los Angeles Film Critics Association Award, Best Supporting Actor (2008); Academy Award, Best Supporting Actor (2009); BAFTA Award, Best Supporting Actor (2009); Golden Globe Award, Best Supporting Actor—Motion Picture (2009); Screen Actors Guild Award, Outstanding Performance by a Male Actor in a Supporting Role (2009)

Ledger played a soldier fighting in the American Revolutionary War (1775–1783) in *The Patriot*. He also played a man addicted to heroin in *Candy*.

A CAREER CUT SHORT

In the film *Brokeback Mountain*, Ledger portrayed a cowboy in love with another man. He received an Academy Award nomination for the role. Ledger died in 2008 while filming *The Imaginarium of Doctor Parnassus*. At the time, he had finished filming his role as the Joker in *The Dark Knight*. After his death, Ledger was awarded the Best Supporting Actor Academy Award for his performance in that movie.

The Joker is a villain in the Batman universe. Ledger's portrayal of him was iconic.

BRUCE LEE

Bruce Lee featured in the 1973 movie *Enter the Dragon*, where his character tries to bring down a drug dealer.

Bruce Lee was born on November 27, 1940, in San Francisco, California. He spent his childhood in Hong Kong. When he was around 12, Lee started doing martial arts. He also practiced Western boxing and fencing. As an adult, Lee opened martial arts schools. A film producer noticed Lee's skills, and Lee landed a role in the television series *The Green Hornet*. He began to put his martial arts skills to work in television shows and movies.

A HONG KONG STAR

Lee struggled to get movie roles in Hollywood. So he returned to Hong Kong to act. He starred in the action film *The Big Boss*, playing a student who looks for revenge after his teacher died. Lee also featured in *The Chinese Connection*. His movies were a hit with audiences in both Hong Kong and the United States. Lee's martial arts skills made martial arts films popular in the 1970s. In addition to acting, Lee tried his hand at directing films too.

Lee flies through the air during a stunt in the 1971 film *The Big Boss*.

MELISSA McCARTHY

After high school, Melissa McCarthy performed in comedy clubs in New York City. She landed a role in the popular television series *Gilmore Girls* from 2000 to 2007. In 2010, she got the starring spot in the show *Mike & Molly*. She won an Emmy Award for that role.

A WELL-KNOWN COMEDIAN

In 2012, McCarthy received an Academy Award nomination for her role in the comedy *Bridesmaids*. She has played many characters during her career. McCarthy was a scam artist in *Identity Thief* and a police officer in the comedy *The Heat*. In 2017, McCarthy won an Emmy Award for her role on

Melissa McCarthy received a star on the Hollywood Walk of Fame in 2015. Hers was the 2,552nd star.

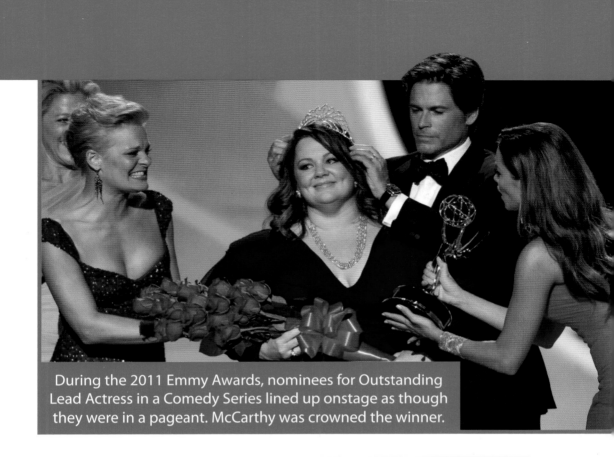

During the 2011 Emmy Awards, nominees for Outstanding Lead Actress in a Comedy Series lined up onstage as though they were in a pageant. McCarthy was crowned the winner.

Saturday Night Live when she impersonated Sean Spicer, President Donald Trump's press secretary. McCarthy's second Academy Award nomination came for her role in *Can You Ever Forgive Me?* In that film, she played a celebrity biographer who has fallen out of favor.

AT A GLANCE

Notable Films: *Bridesmaids* (2011), *Identity Thief* (2013), *The Heat* (2013), *St. Vincent* (2014), *Tammy* (2014), *Spy* (2015), *Ghostbusters* (2016), *The Boss* (2016), *Can You Ever Forgive Me?* (2018), *Thunder Force* (2021)

Notable Awards: Emmy Awards, Outstanding Lead Actress in a Comedy Series (2011), Outstanding Guest Actress in a Comedy Series (2017)

FRANCES McDORMAND

Frances McDormand studied theater in college and then moved to New York City to pursue her acting career. Her first film role was in the crime movie *Blood Simple*. In this film, McDormand plays the adulterous wife of a bar owner.

ACTING AND PRODUCING MOVIES

McDormand received an Academy Award nomination for her acting in *Mississippi Burning*. She later won the Best Actress Academy Award for her role as the sheriff in *Fargo*. McDormand won her second Academy Award for playing a mother trying to find

Frances McDormand realized her love for acting when she starred in a play while in high school.

her daughter's killer in *Three Billboards Outside Ebbing, Missouri*. She also starred in and produced the film *Nomadland*, which told the story of a woman who loses her home and then travels across the United States looking for work. For *Nomadland*, McDormand received a third Academy Award for Best Actress and also an Academy Award as a producer. This made her the first female actor to be recognized for both producing and acting in a single year.

AT A GLANCE

Notable Films: *Blood Simple* (1984), *Raising Arizona* (1987), *Mississippi Burning* (1988), *Fargo* (1996), *Almost Famous* (2000), *Wonder Boys* (2000), *Moonrise Kingdom* (2012), *Three Billboards Outside Ebbing, Missouri* (2017), *Nomadland* (2020), *The Tragedy of Macbeth* (2021)

Notable Awards: Screen Actors Guild Awards, Outstanding Performance by a Female Actor in a Leading Role (1997), Outstanding Performance by a Female Actor in a Television Movie or Miniseries (2015), Outstanding Performance by a Female Actor in a Leading Role (2018); Academy Awards, Best Actress (1997, 2018, 2021), Best Motion Picture of the Year (2021); BAFTA Awards, Best Leading Actress (2018, 2021), Best Film (2021); Golden Globe Award, Best Actress—Motion Picture, Drama (2018)

McDormand's character goes face-to-face with law enforcement in *Three Billboards Outside Ebbing, Missouri.*

LIZA MINNELLI

Liza Minnelli, *second from right*, holds her first Tony Award, which she won in 1965.

Liza Minnelli's parents were actor Judy Garland and film director Vincente Minnelli. Liza landed a role in the off-Broadway musical *Best Foot Forward* in 1963. Two years later, she appeared in the musical *Flora, the Red Menace*. She was 19 years old at the time. Minnelli earned a Tony Award for Best Actress in a Musical.

BREAKING INTO FILMS

Minnelli's first movie was *Charlie Bubbles*, where she played a minor role as a secretary. It was her performance in the romantic comedy *The Sterile Cuckoo* that brought Minnelli her first Academy Award nomination for Best Actress. Her most famous film role was in the musical *Cabaret*, where she played a singer at a nightclub. Minnelli won a Best Actress Academy Award for her performance. While acting in films, Minnelli also performed as a singer and in Broadway plays. She received a Special Tony Award in 1974. Four years later, she won another Tony Award for her role in the Broadway musical *The Act*.

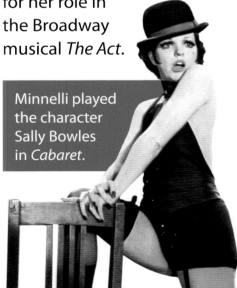

Minnelli played the character Sally Bowles in *Cabaret*.

The first 15 years of Helen Mirren's career were spent with the Royal Shakespeare Company in England. This theatrical group often performs plays written by William Shakespeare. Mirren starred in plays such as *Troilus and Cressida* and *Antony and Cleopatra*.

CRITICAL PRAISE

Mirren has not only had success on the stage but she's also been praised for her film and television roles. Mirren acted in movies such as *The Long Good Friday*, *Excalibur*, and *Cal* in the 1980s. With her role as Queen Charlotte in *The Madness of King George*, she received a Best Supporting Actress Academy Award nomination.

Helen Mirren was born in England. When she was 18 years old, Mirren began performing in the National Youth Theatre.

The Queen dramatizes historical events from 1997 after Princess Diana—the queen's former daughter-in-law—dies.

She received two more Academy Award nominations for *Gosford Park* and *The Last Station*. She won an Academy Award for Best Actress for her role as Queen Elizabeth II in *The Queen*. Mirren also won awards for her role as a detective in the television series *Prime Suspect*, which ran for seven seasons.

AT A GLANCE

Notable Films: *Excalibur* (1981), *The Long Good Friday* (1982), *Cal* (1984), *The Madness of King George* (1994), *Gosford Park* (2001), *The Queen* (2006), *The Last Station* (2009), *RED* (2010), *Hitchcock* (2012), *Eye in the Sky* (2015)

Notable Awards: BAFTA Awards, Best Actress (1992, 1993, 1994, 2007); Emmy Awards, Outstanding Lead Actress in a Miniseries or a Special (1996, 1999, 2006, 2007); Golden Globe Awards, Best Actress—Limited Series, Anthology Series, or Television Motion Picture (1997, 2007), Best Actress—Motion Picture, Drama (2007); Academy Award, Best Actress (2007)

Marilyn Monroe was born Norma Jeane Mortenson on June 1, 1926, in Los Angeles, California. After getting her first studio contract in 1946, she changed her name to Marilyn Monroe. She also dyed her hair blond.

FILM CAREER

Monroe played a small role in the movie *All about Eve*, which brought her some fame. Her starring role in *Niagara* propelled her to fame. The Hollywood film studios advertised her blond bombshell image.

Marilyn Monroe died in 1962 at the age of 36.

Monroe starred with Tom Ewell in *The Seven Year Itch*.

Monroe's popularity rose further after featuring in films like *Gentlemen Prefer Blondes* and *How to Marry a Millionaire*. Monroe was well known around the world. She ran her own film company called Marilyn Monroe Productions. Her skill as a comedian was shown in films like *The Seven Year Itch* and *Bus Stop*. Critics praised her acting skills in *Some Like It Hot*.

AT A GLANCE

Notable Films: *All about Eve* (1950), *The Asphalt Jungle* (1950), *Niagara* (1953), *How to Marry a Millionaire* (1953), *Gentlemen Prefer Blondes* (1953), *There's No Business like Show Business* (1954), *The Seven Year Itch* (1955), *Bus Stop* (1956), *Some Like It Hot* (1959), *The Misfits* (1961)

Notable Awards: Golden Globe Awards, World Film Favorites (1954, 1962), Best Actress—Musical/Comedy (1960)

In 1980, Eddie Murphy joined the cast of the popular comedy show *Saturday Night Live*. He was 19 years old. He soon rose to prominence on the show with his acting and humor.

STARRING IN POPULAR FILMS

Murphy's first film was *48 Hrs.*, and it was a huge hit. Other popular movies such as *Trading Places* and *Beverly Hills Cop* soon followed. The critics praised Murphy's work in playing multiple characters in the movie *Coming to America*. His family-friendly films *The Nutty Professor* and *Dr. Dolittle* were well-received too. Murphy was the voice actor for the role of Donkey in the *Shrek* films in the early 2000s. He received an Academy Award nomination for Best Supporting Actor for his role in the musical *Dreamgirls*. Murphy returned to *Saturday Night Live* as the host in 2019.

SATURDAY NIGHT LIVE

Saturday Night Live is a popular comedy television show. It has won numerous Emmy Awards over the years. Many comedians who started acting on *Saturday Night Live* have gone on to highly successful acting careers.

Eddie Murphy received the Cecil B. DeMille Award at the 2023 Golden Globes.

In *Dr. Dolittle*, Murphy plays a doctor who can speak with animals.

He received an Emmy Award for his performance. In 2015, the Kennedy Center honored him with the Mark Twain Prize for American Humor.

AT A GLANCE

Notable Films: *48 Hrs.* (1982), *Trading Places* (1983), *Beverly Hills Cop* (1984), *The Golden Child* (1986), *Coming to America* (1988), *The Nutty Professor* (1996), *Mulan* (1998), *Shrek* (2001), *Shrek 2* (2004), *Dreamgirls* (2006), *Tower Heist* (2011)

Notable Awards: Grammy Award, Best Comedy Recording (1984); Screen Actors Guild Award, Outstanding Performance by a Male Actor in a Supporting Role (2007); Golden Globe Awards, Best Supporting Actor—Motion Picture (2007), Cecil B. DeMille Award (2023); Kennedy Center, Mark Twain Prize for American Humor (2015); Emmy Award, Outstanding Guest Actor in a Comedy Series (2020)

BILL MURRAY

Bill Murray became known for his humor on the comedy show *Saturday Night Live*. His early films, *Meatballs*, *Caddyshack*, and *Stripes*, were comedies. In 1984, Murray starred in the highly popular film *Ghostbusters*. Murray received a Best Actor Academy Award nomination for his role in the comedy drama *Lost in Translation*. In that film, he played an aging actor. Murray received the Kennedy Center's Mark Twain Prize for American Humor in 2016.

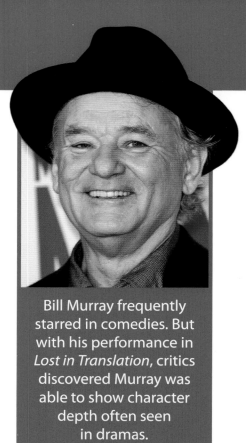

Bill Murray frequently starred in comedies. But with his performance in *Lost in Translation*, critics discovered Murray was able to show character depth often seen in dramas.

AT A GLANCE

Notable Films: *Tootsie* (1982), *Ghostbusters* (1984), *Groundhog Day* (1993), *Ed Wood* (1994), *Rushmore* (1998), *The Royal Tenenbaums* (2001), *Lost in Translation* (2003), *The Life Aquatic with Steve Zissou* (2004), *Moonrise Kingdom* (2012), *The Grand Budapest Hotel* (2014), *Isle of Dogs* (2018)

Notable Awards: Golden Globe Award, Best Actor—Motion Picture, Musical/Comedy (2004); Emmy Awards, Outstanding Supporting Actor in a Limited Series or a Movie (2015), Outstanding Writing in a Comedy-Variety or Music Series (1977); Kennedy Center, Mark Twain Prize for American Humor (2016)

PAUL NEWMAN

Paul Newman was born on January 26, 1925, in Cleveland, Ohio. Newman studied acting in college and served in World War II. His first Broadway role was in *Picnic* in 1953. With his part as a boxer in the film *Somebody Up There Likes Me* in 1956, Newman's fame rose. He received 12 Academy Award nominations and won Best Actor for his role in *The Color of Money*. Critics and fans consider Newman to be an acting legend, and his career lasted more than 50 years. Newman died in 2008.

AT A GLANCE

Notable Films: *Somebody Up There Likes Me* (1956), *Cat on a Hot Tin Roof* (1958), *The Hustler* (1961), *Cool Hand Luke* (1967), *Butch Cassidy and the Sundance Kid* (1969), *The Sting* (1973), *Absence of Malice* (1981), *The Verdict* (1982), *The Color of Money* (1986), *Nobody's Fool* (1994)

Notable Awards: Golden Globe Awards, Most Promising Newcomer (1957), World Film Favorite (1964, 1966), Cecil B. DeMille Award (1984), Best Supporting Actor— Television (2006); BAFTA Award, Best Foreign Actor (1962); Screen Actors Guild Awards, Life Achievement Award (1986), Outstanding Performance by a Male Actor in a Television Movie or Miniseries (2006); Academy Awards, Honorary Award (1986), Best Actor (1987), Jean Hersholt Humanitarian Award (1994)

Paul Newman directed movies including *Rachel, Rachel* (1968) and *Sometimes a Great Notion* (1971).

JACK NICHOLSON

Jack Nicholson was born in New Jersey, but after high school he moved to Los Angeles. He began working in stage plays and appearing in small television roles. He spent most of the 1960s acting in B-films, along with some television roles.

A BIG BREAK

Nicholson's big break as an actor came with the film *Easy Rider*. He was nominated for an Academy Award for his role in this counterculture film. In it,

Jack Nicholson's character in *The Shining* goes mad and breaks through part of a door with an axe.

B-FILMS

B-films are low-budget movies. During the 1930s and 1940s, theaters often showed two full-length films back-to-back. These double features were a way of drawing more people to the theater. Typically the double feature was an A-film, or the main attraction, paired with a B-film. A-films were the better quality, bigger-budget films. The term *B-film* is still often used to describe a poor-quality, cheaply made movie.

he played a lawyer with a substance use disorder. Nicholson's portrayal of a private detective in *Chinatown* is considered by many film critics to be his finest performance. For his role as a patient in a mental institution in *One Flew over the Cuckoo's Nest*, he won an Academy Award. One of Nicholson's most memorable roles was in the horror film *The Shining*. In it, he played a hotel caretaker who loses his mind. Nicholson won two more Academy Awards for *Terms of Endearment* and *As Good as It Gets*.

Nicholson's character J. J. Gittes must navigate corruption, lies, and murder in *Chinatown*.

Lupita Nyong'o grew up in Kenya. While going to Hampshire College in Massachusetts, Nyong'o focused on both African studies and film. She even worked on several movie sets as an intern and production assistant. She went on to get a master's degree at Yale School of Drama.

A STRONG START

Nyong'o landed her first significant movie role in *12 Years a Slave*. She won an Academy Award for Best Supporting Actress for her portrayal of an enslaved woman. Her next film was the action thriller *Non-Stop*. She also played a 1,000-year-old alien in *Star Wars: The Force Awakens* and *Star Wars: The Rise of Skywalker*.

In *Queen of Katwe*, Nyong'o portrayed a Ugandan mother whose daughter is a chess star. She played Nakia, a fighter and activist, in *Black Panther* and

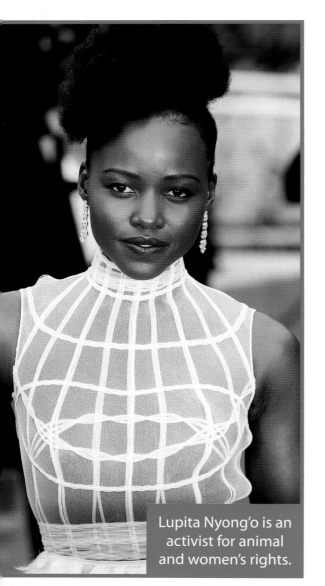

Lupita Nyong'o is an activist for animal and women's rights.

AT A GLANCE

Notable Films: *12 Years a Slave* (2013), *Non-Stop* (2014), *Star Wars* series (2015, 2019), *Queen of Katwe* (2016), *Black Panther* series (2018, 2022), *Us* (2019), *The 355* (2022)

Notable Awards: Los Angeles Film Critics Association Award, Best Supporting Actress (2013); Academy Award, Best Supporting Actress (2014); Screen Actors Guild Award, Outstanding Performance by a Female Actor in a Supporting Role (2014); New York Film Critics Circle Award, Best Actress (2019)

Black Panther: Wakanda Forever. In 2022, she had a role in *The 355*, a spy thriller. Nyong'o has also had success as a stage actor. She made her debut in the Broadway play *Eclipsed* in 2016.

Nyong'o won an Academy Award in 2014.

LAURENCE OLIVIER

Laurence Olivier was born on May 22, 1907, in England. With his acting success both on the stage and in films, many actors and critics view him as the greatest actor of the 1900s. He made his acting debut at age nine in a production of Shakespeare's *Julius Caesar*. People urged Olivier toward an acting career even at that young age. As a young adult, Olivier had successful performances in plays in London's West End theater district.

Laurence Olivier played Hamlet in the 1948 film of the same name.

COMING TO HOLLYWOOD

By the early 1930s, Olivier had moved to Los Angeles to take on movie roles. He received

DID YOU KNOW?

In 1970, Laurence Olivier became a member of the House of Lords in the UK Parliament. He was the first actor to receive this honor. He received the title Lord Olivier.

Heathcliff was a vengeful character.

an Academy Award nomination for his role as Heathcliff in *Wuthering Heights*. His fame in the United States rose. Olivier was known for his roles in films of Shakespeare's plays. He starred in and directed *Hamlet*, winning an Academy Award for Best Actor and Best Picture.

AL PACINO

In 1969, Al Pacino landed his first film role and made his debut in a Broadway play. His first leading role in a film was in *The Panic in Needle Park* in 1971. A year later, he appeared in *The Godfather*. In that movie, he played

The director of *The Godfather* sought out Al Pacino to play the role of Michael Corleone.

AT A GLANCE

Notable Films: *The Godfather* series (1972, 1974, 1990), *Serpico* (1973), *Dog Day Afternoon* (1975), *Scarface* (1983), *Scent of a Woman* (1992), *Heat* (1995), *The Insider* (1999), *Insomnia* (2002), *Ocean's Thirteen* (2007), *The Irishman* (2019)

Notable Awards: Golden Globe Awards, Best Actor—Motion Picture, Drama (1974, 1993), Cecil B. DeMille Award (2001), Best Actor—Limited Series, Anthology Series, or Television Motion Picture (2004, 2011); BAFTA Award, Best Actor (1976); Academy Award, Best Actor (1993); Emmy Awards, Outstanding Lead Actor in a Miniseries or a Movie (2004, 2010); American Film Institute, Life Achievement Award (2007)

the son of a gangster. Pacino's role in this popular film made him a star.

MOVIES, TELEVISION, AND PLAYS

Following *The Godfather*, Pacino had roles in several other successful movies, such as *Serpico* and *Dog Day Afternoon*. He also appeared in *The Godfather, Part II* and *The Godfather, Part III*. His portrayal of a blind man in *Scent of a Woman* earned him an Academy Award for Best Actor. Besides his movie roles, Pacino has had success in television and plays. He earned an Emmy Award and Golden Globe Award for his television roles and a Tony Award for his acting onstage.

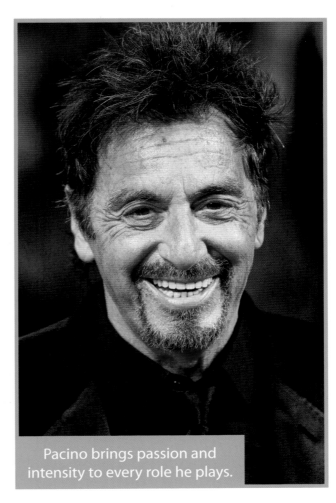

Pacino brings passion and intensity to every role he plays.

Joaquin Phoenix's acting career started with roles in television commercials and then television shows. His first movie roles were in *SpaceCamp* and *Parenthood*. Phoenix received an Academy Award nomination for Best Supporting Actor in *Gladiator*. In that film, he played the Roman emperor Commodus. Phoenix appeared in other well-received movies in the early 2000s including *Quills*, *Signs*, and *Hotel Rwanda*.

BECOMING THE CHARACTER

Phoenix has a reputation for fully immersing himself in the characters he plays. For instance, when preparing for his role as musician Johnny Cash in *Walk the Line*, Phoenix had special vocal training in order to perform Cash's songs. He received high praise for his singing and acting in the film. He got another Academy Award nomination for his portrayal of Cash. Phoenix's third Academy

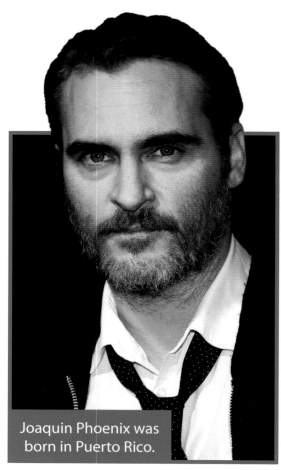

Joaquin Phoenix was born in Puerto Rico.

Phoenix, *left*, won a Golden Globe in 2006 for his performance in *Walk the Line*.

Award nomination came after his performance in *The Master*. It was for his role as the Joker in the film *Joker* that he won the Academy Award for Best Actor.

AT A GLANCE

Notable Films: *Parenthood* (1989), *To Die For* (1995), *Gladiator* (2000), *Hotel Rwanda* (2004), *Walk the Line* (2005), *The Master* (2012), *Her* (2013), *Inherent Vice* (2014), *You Were Never Really Here* (2017), *Joker* (2019)

Notable Awards: Golden Globe Awards, Best Actor—Motion Picture, Musical/Comedy (2006), Best Actor—Motion Picture, Drama (2020); Grammy Award, Best Compilation Soundtrack Album for Motion Picture, Television, or Other Visual Media (2007); Los Angeles Film Critics Association Award, Best Actor (2012); Cannes Film Festival, Best Actor (2017); Academy Award, Best Actor (2020); BAFTA Award, Best Leading Actor (2020)

BRAD PITT

In 1991, Brad Pitt appeared in a minor role in the popular movie *Thelma & Louise* and caught the attention of audiences. Four years later, in *12 Monkeys*, Pitt played a patient in a mental institution. His performance earned him a Golden Globe Award. He was also nominated for a Best Supporting Actor Academy Award.

TACKLING DIFFERENT ROLES

Pitt played a mountain climber in *Seven Years in Tibet*. He was a terrorist in *The Devil's Own*. He acted as an underground boxer in *Fight Club*. In 2001, he starred in the comedy film *Ocean's Eleven*. Pitt went on to perform in two additional *Ocean's* movies as well. He received two more Best Actor Academy Award nominations for his roles in *The Curious Case of Benjamin Button* and *Moneyball*. He won the Best Supporting Actor Academy Award for the film *Once Upon a Time . . . in Hollywood*.

Brad Pitt is one of the most well-known stars in Hollywood.

AT A GLANCE

Notable Films: *Thelma & Louise* (1991), *12 Monkeys* (1995), *Se7en* (1995), *Fight Club* (1999), *Ocean's Eleven* (2001), *The Assassination of Jesse James by the Coward Robert Ford* (2007), *Burn After Reading* (2008), *The Curious Case of Benjamin Button* (2008), *Moneyball* (2011), *12 Years a Slave* (2013), *Ad Astra* (2019), *Once Upon a Time . . . in Hollywood* (2019), *Babylon* (2022)

Notable Awards: Golden Globe Awards, Best Supporting Actor—Motion Picture (1996, 2020); New York Film Critics Circle Award, Best Actor (2011); Emmy Award, Outstanding Television Movie (2014); BAFTA Awards, Best Film (2014), Best Supporting Actor (2020); National Board of Review, Best Supporting Actor (2019); Screen Actors Guild Award, Outstanding Performance by a Male Actor in a Supporting Role (2020); Academy Award, Best Supporting Actor (2020)

In his Academy Award acceptance speech, Pitt thanked the director of *Once Upon a Time . . . in Hollywood*, Quentin Tarantino.

SIDNEY POITIER

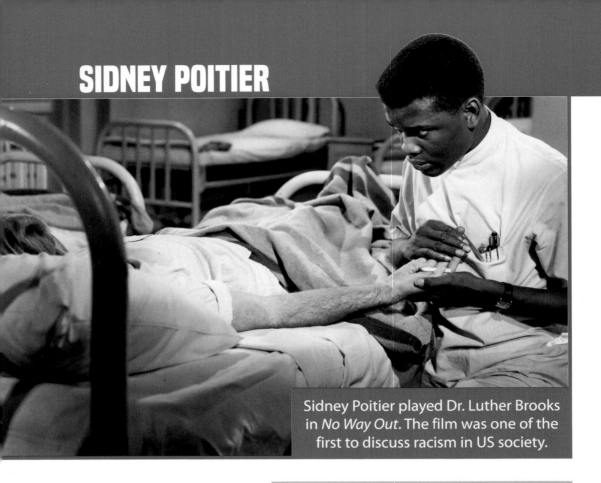

Sidney Poitier played Dr. Luther Brooks in *No Way Out*. The film was one of the first to discuss racism in US society.

Sidney Poitier carefully chose his film roles. At the time, Hollywood often cast Black people in demeaning roles. They played the parts of enslaved people, criminals, or people who took care of white children.

AMERICA IN THE 1950s AND 1960s

The civil rights movement of the 1950s and 1960s took place as Poitier rose to fame. The movement focused on eliminating racial discrimination and segregation in the United States. Black people worked to gain the same rights as white people. Poitier's careful selection of film roles focused on showing Black people in a positive, nonstereotypical light. He also actively supported the civil rights movement.

Poitier didn't want to promote harmful stereotypes about Black people by accepting jobs like that. He played only characters with substance. He was a doctor in *No Way Out*. In the movie *Cry, the Beloved Country*, Poitier played a minister. His films *Edge of the City* and *Band of Angels* both explored topics of racial tension. In the

movie *Guess Who's Coming to Dinner*, Poitier played a doctor who was engaged to a white woman. At the time, interracial marriage was illegal in some states, and the movie caused a stir.

WINNING AN ACADEMY AWARD

Poitier received an Academy Award nomination for his performance in *The Defiant Ones*. This film promoted racial harmony. Poitier won the Best Actor Academy Award for his role in *Lilies of the Field*. It was the first time a Black man had won an Academy Award.

Natalie Portman's first movie role was in *Léon: The Professional*. Portman's roles have been wide-ranging. She acted in the musical *Everyone Says I Love You* and in the alien-invasion comedy *Mars Attacks!* She also played Queen Amidala in *Star Wars: Episode I—The Phantom Menace*. She took on this role again in the film's two sequels.

THE ACADEMY AWARDS

Portman received her first Academy Award nomination and a Golden Globe Award for Best Supporting Actress for *Closer*. She won the Best Actress Academy Award for her portrayal of a troubled ballet dancer in *Black Swan*. She played former first lady Jacqueline Kennedy in the film *Jackie*. Portman received an Academy Award nomination for her performance.

Natalie Portman was born in Israel. Her family moved to the United States when she was a child.

140

To prepare for her role in *Black Swan*, Portman spent hours each day dancing.

AT A GLANCE

Notable Films: *Léon: The Professional* (1994), *Heat* (1995), *Beautiful Girls* (1996), *Star Wars* series (1999, 2002, 2005), *Garden State* (2004), *Closer* (2004), *V for Vendetta* (2005), *Black Swan* (2010), *Jackie* (2016), *Vox Lux* (2018), *Annihilation* (2018)

Notable Awards: Golden Globe Awards, Best Supporting Actress—Motion Picture (2005), Best Actress—Motion Picture, Drama (2011); Academy Award, Best Actress (2011); BAFTA Award, Best Leading Actress (2011); Screen Actors Guild Award, Outstanding Performance by a Female Actor in a Leading Role (2011)

MARGOT ROBBIE

Margot Robbie began acting in television and film as a teenager, but she achieved her breakthrough role in the 2013 movie *The Wolf of Wall Street*. In 2016, Robbie played Harley Quinn in *Suicide Squad*. She would play the character again in 2020 and 2021 in *Birds of Prey* and *The Suicide Squad*, respectively. She earned her first Academy Award nomination in 2018 for her leading role as figure skater Tonya Harding in *I, Tonya*. Her second came in 2020 for her supporting role as a TV producer in *Bombshell*. In 2023, she starred alongside actor Ryan Gosling in *Barbie*.

Margot Robbie attended the London, England, premier of *Barbie* on July 12, 2023.

AT A GLANCE

Notable Films: *The Wolf of Wall Street* (2013), *Suicide Squad* (2016), *I, Tonya* (2017), *Mary Queen of Scots* (2018), *Once Upon a Time . . . in Hollywood* (2019), *Bombshell* (2019), *The Suicide Squad* (2021), *Barbie* (2023)

Notable Awards: Critics Choice Awards, Best Actress in an Action Movie (2016), Best Actress in a Comedy (2018); AACTA International Awards, Best Lead Actress (2018), Best Supporting Actress (2020); Alliance of Women Film Journalists' EDA Award, Bravest Performance (2018)

JULIA ROBERTS

From the 1990s through the early 2000s, Julia Roberts was one of the highest-paid female actors.

In 1989, Julia Roberts appeared in the movie *Steel Magnolias*. She received a Best Supporting Actress Academy Award nomination. Her role in *Pretty Woman* made her a star. She received a second Academy Award nomination for that film.

Roberts has played many characters. Her starring role in *Erin Brockovich* won her the Academy Award for Best Actress. In that movie, Roberts played the role of a real-life woman who led the fight against a big company that polluted her town's drinking water. Roberts also acted in the popular comedies *Ocean's Eleven* and *Ocean's Twelve*. She received another Academy Award nomination for Best Supporting Actress for her work in the film *August: Osage County*.

AT A GLANCE

Notable Films: *Steel Magnolias* (1989), *Pretty Woman* (1990), *My Best Friend's Wedding* (1997), *Erin Brockovich* (2000), *Ocean's Eleven* (2001), *Closer* (2004), *August: Osage County* (2013)

Notable Awards: Golden Globe Awards, Best Supporting Actress—Motion Picture (1990), Best Actress—Motion Picture, Musical/Comedy (1991), Best Actress—Motion Picture, Drama (2001); Academy Award, Best Actress (2001); BAFTA Award, Best Performance by an Actress in a Leading Role (2001)

ZOE SALDANA

When she was a teenager, Zoe Saldana moved to New York City to perform with theater groups. She landed a role in the television series *Law & Order*. Next, she got a part in the movie *Center Stage*. It told the story of student in a New York City ballet school.

A SCIENCE-FICTION STAR

In the early 2000s, Saldana appeared in several films that appealed to teen audiences. These included *Get Over It*, *Crossroads*, and *Drumline*. Then she played a female pirate in the hit movie *Pirates of the Caribbean: The Curse of the Black Pearl*.

Saldana is known for playing strong female roles in science-fiction films. She was Lieutenant Uhura in the *Star Trek* series. In *Avatar*, she played the character Neytiri.

Zoe Saldana is a strong supporter of making Hollywood more diverse.

Saldana's character in *Star Trek* is a communications officer on a starship.

She also played the warrior Gamora in the *Guardians of the Galaxy* and *Avengers* series.

Saldana has starred in many box-office hits. She became the first person to feature in four movies that made more than $2 billion. The films were *Avatar*, *Avengers: Endgame*, *Avengers: Infinity War*, and *Avatar: The Way of Water*.

AT A GLANCE

Notable Films: *Pirates of the Caribbean: The Curse of the Black Pearl* (2003), *Star Trek* series (2009, 2013, 2016), *Avatar* series (2009, 2022), *Colombiana* (2011), *Guardians of the Galaxy* (2014), *The Losers* (2010), *Avengers* series (2018, 2019)

Notable Awards: Academy of Science Fiction, Fantasy & Horror Films, Best Actress (2010); Empire Award, Best Actress (2010); ALMA Award, Favorite Movie Actress—Drama/Adventure (2012)

ADAM SANDLER

Adam Sandler started performing stand-up comedy when he was 17. He wrote and performed for the popular comedy show *Saturday Night Live*. He starred in and cowrote the comedy film *Billy Madison*. Some critics thought his humor and characters were immature, but Sandler was popular with movie audiences.

Critics have said Adam Sandler's humor is childish, but audiences have flocked to his movies.

AT A GLANCE

Notable Films: *Billy Madison* (1995), *Happy Gilmore* (1996), *The Wedding Singer* (1998), *The Waterboy* (1998), *Punch-Drunk Love* (2002), *Spanglish* (2004), *Reign Over Me* (2007), *The Meyerowitz Stories* (2017), *Uncut Gems* (2019), *Hustle* (2022)

Notable Awards: People's Choice Awards, Favorite Motion Picture Star in a Comedy (2000), Favorite On-Screen Chemistry (2005), Favorite Funny Male Star (2006, 2009), Favorite Comedic Star (2011), Favorite Comedic Movie Actor (2012, 2013, 2014, 2015); National Board of Review, Best Actor (2019); Kennedy Center, Mark Twain Prize for American Humor (2023)

PRODUCING AND ACTING

Sandler formed his own production company in 1999. With this, he began both producing and acting in his film projects. Sandler starred in *Punch-Drunk Love*. Critics praised his work, and he was nominated for a Best Actor Golden Globe Award. In 2023, Sandler was awarded the Kennedy Center's Mark Twain Prize for American Humor.

DID YOU KNOW?

When movies or plays combine elements of drama and comedy, they are sometimes called dramedies. Some of Sandler's films—*Funny People*, *Grown Ups*, and *Just Go with It*—are dramedies.

Sandler accepts his 2015 People's Choice Award.

SUSAN SARANDON

Susan Sarandon has received nine Golden Globe nominations.

Susan Sarandon studied drama in college before landing some television acting roles. She appeared in the popular film *The Rocky Horror Picture Show*. Sarandon received her first Academy Award nomination for her role as a waitress in the crime-drama *Atlantic City*. Her acting in the popular romantic comedy *Bull Durham*, where she played a baseball groupie, made Sarandon a star. She won the Academy Award for Best Actress for her performance in *Dead Man Walking*. In that movie, Sarandon played the role of Sister Helen Prejean, a nun who tries to abolish the death penalty.

AT A GLANCE

Notable Films: *The Rocky Horror Picture Show* (1975), *Pretty Baby* (1978), *Atlantic City* (1980), *The Witches of Eastwick* (1987), *Bull Durham* (1988), *Thelma & Louise* (1991), *Lorenzo's Oil* (1992), *The Client* (1994), *Little Women* (1994), *Dead Man Walking* (1995)

Notable Awards: National Board of Review, Best Actress (1991); BAFTA Award, Best Actress (1995); Academy Award, Best Actress (1996); Screen Actors Guild Award, Outstanding Performance by a Female Actor in a Leading Role (1996); Cannes Film Festival Award, Kering Women in Motion Award (2016)

MAGGIE SMITH

Maggie Smith's first Academy Award came for her performance as a schoolteacher in *The Prime of Miss Jean Brodie*. Her second was for playing an actress in *California Suite*. Smith also starred in the highly popular *Harry Potter* movies. She was in the television series *Downton Abbey* too.

Maggie Smith was born on December 28, 1934, in England.

AT A GLANCE

Notable Films: *The Prime of Miss Jean Brodie* (1969), *California Suite* (1978), *A Room with a View* (1985), *Gosford Park* (2001), *Harry Potter* series (2001, 2002, 2004, 2005, 2007, 2009, 2011), *The Best Exotic Marigold Hotel* (2011), *Quartet* (2012)

Notable Awards: Academy Awards, Best Actress (1970), Best Supporting Actress (1979); Golden Globe Awards, Best Actress—Motion Picture, Musical/Comedy (1979), Best Supporting Actress—Motion Picture (1987); Emmy Awards, Outstanding Lead Actress in a Miniseries or a Movie (2003), Outstanding Supporting Actress in a Miniseries or Movie (2011), Outstanding Supporting Actress in a Drama Series (2012, 2016); Tony Award, Best Actress (1990)

DID YOU KNOW?

Maggie Smith has won the triple crown of acting, meaning she has an Academy Award, a Tony Award, and an Emmy Award.

WILL SMITH

In high school, Will Smith and his friend began performing rap music. Smith was known as the Fresh Prince. He won a Grammy Award for the song "Parents Just Don't Understand." Starting in 1990, Smith starred in the popular comedy television show *The Fresh Prince of Bel-Air*.

ACTING CAREER TAKES OFF

Following his success with *The Fresh Prince of Bel-Air*, Smith began acting in films. He starred in *Independence Day*. He then got a role in the popular science-fiction film *Men in Black*. He played a golfer in *The Legend of Bagger Vance*. Then Smith played the boxer Muhammad Ali in the film *Ali* and received an

Will Smith acted in *The Fresh Prince of Bel-Air* for all six of its seasons.

Smith and his wife, Jada Pinkett Smith, got married in 1997. They have two children together, and Smith has a son from a previous marriage too.

AT A GLANCE

Notable Films: *Where the Day Takes You* (1992), *Six Degrees of Separation* (1993), *Independence Day* (1996), *Men in Black* series (1997, 2002, 2012), *Enemy of the State* (1998), *Ali* (2001), *The Pursuit of Happyness* (2006), *I Am Legend* (2007), *Bad Boys for Life* (2020), *King Richard* (2021)

Notable Awards: Academy Award, Best Actor (2022); BAFTA Award, Best Leading Actor (2022); Golden Globe Award, Best Actor—Motion Picture, Drama (2022); National Board of Review, Best Actor (2021); Screen Actors Guild Award, Outstanding Performance by a Male Actor in a Leading Role (2022)

Academy Award nomination. Smith got a second Academy Award nomination for Best Actor in *The Pursuit of Happyness*, where he played a single dad. Smith won the Best Actor Academy Award for his role as the father of tennis players Venus and Serena Williams in *King Richard*.

Octavia Spencer worked in casting departments for film companies before pursuing television and movie roles herself. Her big break came when she got the role of the outspoken housemaid Minny Jackson in *The Help*. The film focuses on race relations in Mississippi in the 1960s. Spencer won the Best Supporting Actress Academy Award for her performance.

Octavia Spencer poses for the cameras after winning her Academy Award in 2012.

LEADING ROLES

Spencer played the aunt of singer James Brown in the film *Get On Up*. In the popular animated film *Zootopia*, Spencer was the voice actor for the character Mrs. Otterton. In *Hidden Figures*, she played the role of Dorothy Vaughan. Vaughan was a computer programmer who worked for the US National Aeronautics and Space Administration (NASA) during the late 1950s. Spencer received

Spencer's character in *Hidden Figures* was based on a real person named Dorothy Vaughan. Spencer tried to portray Vaughan as truthfully as possible.

an Academy Award nomination for this role. She got another Academy Award nomination for her performance in *The Shape of Water*. In this movie, Spencer played a member of the janitorial staff at a government lab.

AT A GLANCE

Notable Films: *The Help* (2011), *Smashed* (2012), *Snowpiercer* (2013), *Fruitvale Station* (2013), *Get On Up* (2014), *Zootopia* (2016), *Hidden Figures* (2016), *Small Town Crime* (2017), *The Shape of Water* (2017), *Instant Family* (2018)

Notable Awards: Academy Award, Best Supporting Actress (2012); Golden Globe Award, Best Supporting Actress—Motion Picture (2012); Screen Actors Guild Award, Outstanding Performance by a Female Actor in a Supporting Role (2012); BAFTA Award, Best Supporting Actress (2012); National Board of Review, Best Supporting Actress (2013)

JAMES STEWART

James Stewart was known for his roles as an ordinary guy pulled into a crisis. Also called Jimmy Stewart, he was praised for his role as a senator fighting corruption in *Mr. Smith Goes to Washington*. That film earned him a Best Actor Academy Award nomination. His performance as a reporter in *The Philadelphia Story* won him the Best Actor Academy Award.

SERVING HIS COUNTRY

When the United States entered World War II, Stewart joined the US Army, serving as a pilot. After the war, he starred in *It's a Wonderful Life* and got a third Academy Award nomination. Stewart played a struggling banker in the movie.

James Stewart, *right*, made waves for his part in *Mr. Smith Goes to Washington*. Audiences praised the movie, but politicians were upset with it.

As an older actor, Stewart took on more serious roles. Some movies he featured in included *Rear Window*, *Vertigo*, *Winchester '73*, and *The Glenn Miller Story*. He received another Academy Award nomination for his work as a lawyer in *Anatomy of a Murder*.

Stewart joined the war effort in 1940. He flew bomber planes over Europe.

AT A GLANCE

Notable Films: *Mr. Smith Goes to Washington* (1939), *The Philadelphia Story* (1940), *It's a Wonderful Life* (1946), *Winchester '73* (1950), *Harvey* (1950), *Rear Window* (1954), *The Man Who Knew Too Much* (1956), *Vertigo* (1958), *Anatomy of a Murder* (1959), *The Man Who Shot Liberty Valance* (1962)

Notable Awards: New York Film Critics Circle Awards, Best Actor (1939, 1959); National Board of Review, Best Acting (1940), Career Achievement Award (1990); Academy Awards, Best Actor (1941), Honorary Award (1985); Golden Globe Awards, Cecil B. DeMille Award (1965), Best TV Actor—Drama (1974); Screen Actors Guild Award, Life Achievement Award (1969); American Film Institute, Life Achievement Award (1980)

EMMA STONE

As a high school freshman, Emma Stone moved with her mother from Arizona to Los Angeles so Stone could pursue acting. She got some work in television shows. Stone landed a role in the comedy *Superbad*. She also featured in the horror

Emma Stone's first acting role was in 2005, when she appeared in the television show *The New Partridge Family*.

AT A GLANCE

Notable Films: *Zombieland* (2009), *Easy A* (2010), *The Help* (2011), *Crazy, Stupid, Love* (2011), *The Amazing Spider-Man* (2012), *Birdman* (2014), *Magic in the Moonlight* (2014), *La La Land* (2016), *Battle of the Sexes* (2017), *The Favourite* (2018)

Notable Awards: Academy Award, Best Actress (2017); BAFTA Award, Best Leading Actress (2017); Golden Globe Award, Best Actress—Motion Picture, Musical/Comedy (2017); Screen Actors Guild Award, Outstanding Performance by a Female Actor in a Leading Role (2017)

Stone accepts the Academy Award for her performance in *La La Land*, where she played a woman who wants to become an actress.

comedy *Zombieland*. Her first starring role was in *Easy A*. In that movie, she played a high school student who tries to help social outcasts in her school.

MORE THAN COMEDIES

In 2011, Stone played an aspiring writer in *The Help*. Stone also portrayed Spider-Man's girlfriend in the superhero movies *The Amazing Spider-Man* and *The Amazing Spider-Man 2*. She got a Best Supporting Actress Academy Award nomination for her role in *Birdman*, where she played the main character's daughter. With her performance in the musical *La La Land*, Stone won an Academy Award for Best Actress. She received an Academy Award nomination for Best Supporting Actress for *The Favourite*. This historical drama was set in the British queen Anne's court in the early 1700s.

MERYL STREEP

Many film critics and fans call Meryl Streep "the greatest actress." She has received 21 Academy Award nominations and has won the award three times. From her earliest roles in *The Deer Hunter* and *Kramer vs. Kramer*, her brilliant acting skills were evident to film critics. She won a Best Supporting Actress Academy Award for her performance in *Kramer vs. Kramer*.

At first, Meryl Streep appeared in serious dramas. In the 1990s, she started taking more roles in comedies.

WINNING AWARDS

Streep won her second Academy Award for *Sophie's Choice*. This time, it was for Best Actress. In this film, she played a Nazi concentration camp survivor. She earned her third Academy Award

MERYL STREEP'S ACCENTS

Actors often use voice coaches to help them with the accent they need for an upcoming role. Some actors can do the accents better than others. Meryl Streep is known for her talent with accents. For the film *Out of Africa*, she had a Danish accent. For *A Cry in the Dark*, her accent was Australian. In *The Iron Lady*, she spoke perfect British English.

for her role as the former British prime minister Margaret Thatcher in *The Iron Lady*. Streep has also shown her acting skills in comedies and musicals. Some of these include *The Devil Wears Prada*, *Julie & Julia*, *Mama Mia!*, and *Hope Springs*.

Streep holds out her third Academy Award, which she won in 2012.

AT A GLANCE

Notable Films: *The Deer Hunter* (1978), *Kramer vs. Kramer* (1979), *Sophie's Choice* (1982), *Silkwood* (1983), *Postcards from the Edge* (1990), *The Bridges of Madison County* (1995), *The Devil Wears Prada* (2006), *Doubt* (2008), *The Iron Lady* (2011), *Little Women* (2019)

Notable Awards: Emmy Awards, Outstanding Lead Actress in a Limited Series (1978), Outstanding Lead Actress in a Miniseries or a Movie (2004); Academy Awards, Best Supporting Actress (1980), Best Actress (1983, 2012); Golden Globe Award, Cecil B. DeMille Award (2017); BAFTA Awards, Best Actress (1982, 2012); American Film Institute, Life Achievement Award (2004)

WES STUDI

Wes Studi and his wife attend the Academy Awards in 2020.

Wes Studi was born on December 17, 1947, in Nofire Hollow, Oklahoma. Studi spoke his native language, Cherokee, until he started school. He served in the Vietnam War (1954–1975). When Studi returned home from war, he attended college. Then he worked as a professional horse trainer.

AMERICAN INDIANS IN FILM

Into the mid-1900s, Native characters in movies and television shows were often played by non-Native actors. When Native people were cast, they were pushed into stereotypical roles. These roles included the silent, stoic man; the beautiful Native woman whom white men desire; and the savage warrior. Historically, American Indians have been underrepresented in Hollywood. In 2019 and 2020, Native actors were cast in less than 1 percent of television roles.

BREAKING BARRIERS FOR AMERICAN INDIANS

Studi gained the attention of movie critics and fans for his performance in *Dances with Wolves*. His role as the warrior Magua in *The Last of the Mohicans* brought him more fame. Studi also featured in the films *Geronimo: An American Legend* and *Heat*. He appeared in a series of PBS television specials, including *Coyote Waits* and *A Thief of Time*. Throughout his career, Studi has played an important part in bringing well-developed Native characters to the spotlight. In 2019, the Academy of Motion Picture Arts and Sciences presented Studi with the Honorary Award for his lifetime achievement in acting.

Studi, *left*, played an Apache warrior named Geronimo in *Geronimo: An American Legend*.

Elizabeth Taylor was born in England in 1932. Taylor and her parents moved to Los Angeles when she was a child. In 1942, she appeared in her first film, *There's One Born Every Minute*. But it was the movie *National Velvet*, in which Taylor played a girl who saves a horse, that made her famous.

GLAMOROUS AND STRONG-WILLED

As an adult, Taylor often played the role of a glamorous, strong-willed woman. She won a Best Actress Academy Award for her role as a prostitute in *BUtterfield 8*. Taylor received her second Best Actress Academy Award for her performance in *Who's Afraid of Virginia Woolf?* In that movie, Taylor plays a boisterous woman named Martha. In addition to her Academy Awards, Taylor won a Golden Globe for Best Actress after her performance in *Suddenly, Last Summer*. The American Film Institute gave Taylor a Life Achievement Award in 1993.

Elizabeth Taylor had a long, distinguished career before passing away in 2011.

Taylor played Cleopatra in the 1963 movie of the same name. She and her costar Richard Burton, *left*, eventually got married.

AT A GLANCE

Notable Films: *National Velvet* (1944), *Little Women* (1949), *Father of the Bride* (1950), *A Place in the Sun* (1951), *Ivanhoe* (1952), *Giant* (1956), *Cat on a Hot Tin Roof* (1958), *Suddenly, Last Summer* (1959), *BUtterfield 8* (1960), *Cleopatra* (1963), *Who's Afraid of Virginia Woolf?* (1966)

Notable Awards: Golden Globe Awards, Special Award (1957), Best Actress—Drama (1960), World Film Favorite (1974), Cecil B. DeMille Award (1985); Academy Awards, Best Actress (1961, 1967), Jean Hersholt Humanitarian Award (1993); BAFTA Awards, Best British Actress (1967), Academy Fellowship (1999); American Film Institute, Life Achievement Award (1993)

SHIRLEY TEMPLE

Shirley Temple was born on April 23, 1928, in Santa Monica, California. She took dance lessons as a child and was soon appearing in short films. Her first major movie role was *Stand Up and Cheer!* in 1934. That same year, she appeared in the musical *Bright Eyes*, where she sang what would become one of her most popular songs, "On the Good Ship Lollipop." With her bright smile and ringlet curls, audiences loved watching the child star sing and dance. As an adult, Temple left acting and became active in business and politics.

Shirley Temple was known worldwide for her work, and her movies drew in large crowds.

AT A GLANCE

Notable Films: *Bright Eyes* (1934), *The Little Colonel* (1935), *Curly Top* (1935), *The Littlest Rebel* (1935), *Stowaway* (1936), *Captain January* (1936), *Wee Willie Winkie* (1937), *Heidi* (1937), *Rebecca of Sunnybrook Farm* (1938), *The Little Princess* (1939)

Notable Awards: Academy Award, Juvenile Award (1935); National Board of Review, Career Achievement Award (1992); Screen Actors Guild Award, Life Achievement (2006)

CHARLIZE THERON

Charlize Theron grew up in South Africa and studied ballet. She moved to New York City at age 18, where she modeled and studied dance before turning to acting. Her portrayal of a serial killer in the film *Monster* won her the Best Actress Academy Award. Theron immersed herself in that role, gaining almost 30 pounds (14 kg) for the part. She was also highly praised for her role in *North Country*. In that movie, she played a woman leading the fight in a sexual harassment complaint against a large business.

> Charlize Theron lived in Italy for two years as a teen and did modeling work.

AT A GLANCE

Notable Films: *Monster* (2003), *North Country* (2005), *In the Valley of Elah* (2007), *Young Adult* (2011), *Prometheus* (2012), *Mad Max: Fury Road* (2015), *Atomic Blonde* (2017), *Tully* (2018), *Long Shot* (2019), *Bombshell* (2019)

Notable Awards: National Board of Review, Breakthrough Performance by an Actress (2003); Academy Award, Best Actress (2004); Golden Globe Award, Best Actress—Motion Picture, Drama (2004); Screen Actors Guild Award, Outstanding Performance by a Female Actor in a Leading Role (2004)

DENZEL WASHINGTON

Denzel Washington has played many different characters throughout his career.

After college, Denzel Washington began acting in plays in California and New York. His first film role was in the comedy *Carbon Copy* in 1981. Six years later, Washington received an Academy Award nomination for his role as the South African activist Bantu Stephen Biko in the film *Cry Freedom*. When he appeared in the US Civil War drama *Glory*, he won the Academy Award for Best Supporting Actor.

A STRONG PERFORMER

Washington is known for his strong, engaging performances. He often plays the role of real-life people in films. He was the boxer Rubin "Hurricane" Carter in *The Hurricane* and civil rights activist Malcolm X in the film *Malcolm X*. Washington received Academy Award nominations for both of those roles. He won the Academy Award for Best Actor for *Training Day*. In this movie, Washington played a corrupt detective. Washington received the Tony Award for Best Actor for his role in the Broadway drama *Fences*.

Washington holds his Oscar at the 74th Academy Awards in 2002.

AT A GLANCE

Notable Films: *Glory* (1989), *Mississippi Masala* (1991), *Malcolm X* (1992), *The Hurricane* (1999), *Training Day* (2001), *American Gangster* (2007), *Unstoppable* (2010), *Flight* (2012), *Fences* (2016), *The Tragedy of Macbeth* (2021)

Notable Awards: Academy Awards, Best Supporting Actor (1990), Best Actor (2002); Golden Globe Awards, Best Supporting Actor—Motion Picture (1990), Best Actor—Motion Picture, Drama (2000), Cecil B. DeMille Award (2016); New York Film Critics Circle Award, Best Actor (1992); Los Angeles Film Critics Association Award, Best Actor (2001); Screen Actors Guild Award, Outstanding Performance by a Male Actor in a Leading Role (2017)

KEN WATANABE

K en Watanabe was born in Japan. He studied acting in Tokyo in his early twenties. He received praise for his first stage role in the play *Shitaya Mannencho Monogatari*. In 1982, he appeared in his first television show, *Michinaru Hanran*. Next came a film role in *Setouchi Shonen Yakyu Dan* (*MacArthur's Children*) in 1984. He continued to gain fame by starring in Japanese television shows and films.

A CAREER IN HOLLYWOOD

Watanabe's first US film was *The Last Samurai*, where he played a samurai warrior. He received an Academy Award nomination

Ken Watanabe is known for his strong, steady on-screen presence.

In *The Last Samurai*, Watanabe's character works to stop Western influences from changing Japan.

for Best Supporting Actor for his performance. Since then, Watanabe has starred in a variety of roles. In the movie *Batman Begins*, he played the villain Ra's al Ghul. A year later, he portrayed a Japanese war general in *Letters from Iwo Jima*. Watanabe starred in the science-fiction thriller *Inception*. He was also cast as an expert on Japanese monsters called *kaiju* in the *Godzilla* films. In the movie *Tokyo Vice*, Watanabe played a detective.

AT A GLANCE

Notable Films: *The Last Samurai* (2003), *Batman Begins* (2005), *Memoirs of a Geisha* (2005), *Letters from Iwo Jima* (2006), *Inception* (2010), *Godzilla* (2014), *Godzilla: King of the Monsters* (2019)

Notable Awards: Awards of the Japanese Academy, Best Actor (2010, 2021), Best Supporting Actor (2021)

JOHN WAYNE

John Wayne was born May 26, 1907, in Winterset, Iowa. His nickname was "Duke." After college, Wayne got a job at Fox Film Corporation working with stage props. Soon he began to land minor acting roles. His first film playing a leading role was *The Big Trail* in 1930. For the next several years, he acted in movies about cowboys and soldiers.

TRAVELING AND ACTING

During World War II, Wayne traveled overseas with shows that entertained US soldiers. He continued making movies too. In 1956, he starred in *The Searchers* as a man looking for his kidnapped niece.

Wayne earned an Academy Award nomination for one of his military roles,

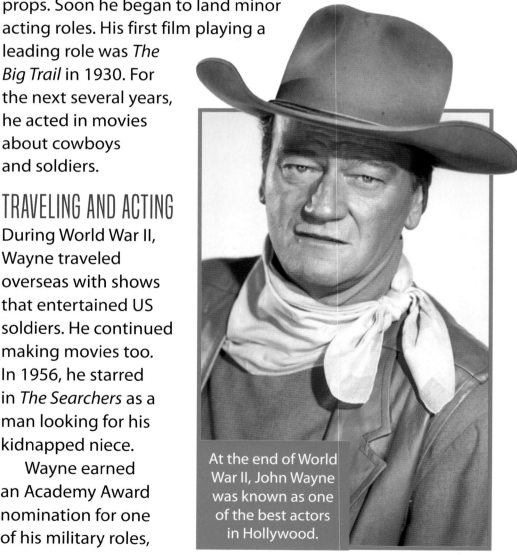

At the end of World War II, John Wayne was known as one of the best actors in Hollywood.

playing a Marine sergeant in *Sands of Iwo Jima*. Wayne won an Academy Award for Best Actor for *True Grit*, where he played a US marshal. His final film role was in *The Shootist*. Many critics consider it to be among his great acting roles.

AT A GLANCE

Notable Films: *Stagecoach* (1939), *The Long Voyage Home* (1940), *They Were Expendable* (1945), *Fort Apache* (1948), *Red River* (1948), *She Wore a Yellow Ribbon* (1949), *The Quiet Man* (1952), *The Searchers* (1956), *The Man Who Shot Liberty Valance* (1962), *True Grit* (1969), *The Shootist* (1976)
Notable Awards: Golden Globe Awards, World Film Favorite (1953), Cecil B. DeMille Award (1966), Best Actor—Drama (1970); Academy Award, Best Actor (1970)

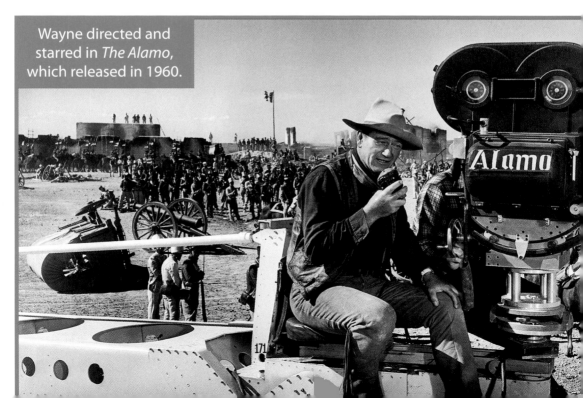

Wayne directed and starred in *The Alamo*, which released in 1960.

171

SIGOURNEY WEAVER

Sigourney Weaver was born on October 8, 1949, in New York City. Her birth name was Susan, but she later changed it to Sigourney after a character in author F. Scott Fitzgerald's novel *The Great Gatsby*. Weaver studied drama in college. The film role that propelled her to fame was in the science-fiction

Sigourney Weaver at the 2023 Academy Awards

horror movie *Alien*. The first *Alien* film led to a series of movies, with Weaver appearing in the first four.

THE QUEEN OF SCI-FI

Weaver earned Academy Award nominations for her performances in *Working Girl, Aliens,* and *Gorillas in the Mist*. She is also known for her roles in *Ghostbusters, The Ice Storm*, and *Holes*. She played Dr. Grace Augustine in *Avatar* and *Avatar: The Way of Water*. Because of her performances in science fiction

Weaver's character in *Avatar* was a skilled scientist.

and fantasy films, Weaver has been given the nickname "Sci-Fi Queen." In addition to her film work, Weaver has also acted in television roles, such as the Netflix series *The Defenders*.

AT A GLANCE

Notable Films: *Alien* series (1979, 1986, 1992, 1997), *The Year of Living Dangerously* (1982), *Ghostbusters* (1984), *Gorillas in the Mist* (1988), *Working Girl* (1988), *Dave* (1993), *The Ice Storm* (1997), *A Map of the World* (1999), *Galaxy Quest* (1999), *Avatar* (2009), *Avatar: The Way of Water* (2022)

Notable Awards: BAFTA Award, Best Performance by an Actress in a Supporting Role (1998); Golden Globe Awards, Best Supporting Actress—Motion Picture (1989), Best Actress—Motion Picture, Drama (1989)

FOREST WHITAKER

Forest Whitaker's first film was the 1982 comedy *Fast Times at Ridgemont High*, in which he had a minor role. For several years, he appeared in television shows such as *Cagney & Lacey* and *Hill Street Blues* before diving back into movies. During the 1990s, Whitaker began directing films. His movies, as both an actor and a director, have been popular with critics and fans. His directing credits include *Waiting to Exhale*, *Hope Floats*, and *First Daughter*.

TAKING ON STRONG CHARACTERS

Whitaker often plays political, military, or law enforcement characters. He also chooses roles where he portrays a historical figure. Movie critics praised Whitaker's performance as the drug-addicted saxophone player Charlie Parker in the film *Bird*.

Forest Whitaker, *left*, poses with his Academy Award in 2007.

Whitaker won an Academy Award for Best Actor when he played the Ugandan dictator Idi Amin in *The Last King of Scotland*.

Whitaker appeared in the superhero movie *Black Panther*, where he played a respected adviser to the king.

AT A GLANCE

Notable Films: *Platoon* (1986), *Good Morning, Vietnam* (1987), *Bird* (1988), *The Crying Game* (1992), *Panic Room* (2002), *Phone Booth* (2002), *The Last King of Scotland* (2006), *The Butler* (2013), *Arrival* (2016), *Rogue One: A Star Wars Story* (2016), *Black Panther* (2018)

Notable Awards: Emmy Award, Outstanding Made for Television Movie (2003); New York Film Critics Circle Award, Best Actor (2006); Academy Award, Best Actor (2007); BAFTA Award, Best Actor in a Leading Role (2007); Golden Globe Award, Best Actor—Motion Picture (2007); Screen Actors Guild Award, Outstanding Performance by a Male Actor in a Leading Role (2007); Cannes Film Festival, Honorary Golden Palm (2022)

Michelle Williams first appeared on the big screen in the film *Lassie* when she was 14 years old. A few years later, she was cast in the popular television series *Dawson's Creek*, playing the role of a rebellious teenager. This role earned the praise of critics and helped launch Williams's acting career.

CRITICAL PRAISE

Williams starred in *Brokeback Mountain*, a story of two cowboys who fall in love. In the film, Williams played the wife of one of the cowboys. Her performance earned her an Academy Award nomination. She got a second nomination for her work in *Blue Valentine*, where she played the role of a woman in a

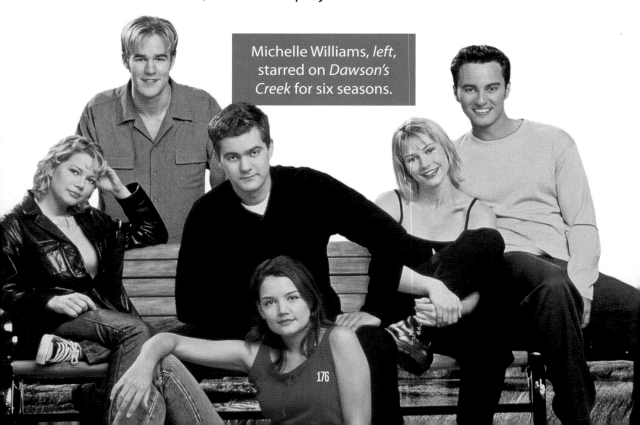

Michelle Williams, *left*, starred on *Dawson's Creek* for six seasons.

176

failing marriage. When Williams played Marilyn Monroe in the film *My Week with Marilyn*, she won a Golden Globe Award for Best Actress and her third Academy Award nomination. Williams also received praise for her role as the main character's ex-wife in *Manchester by the Sea*.

In addition to acting in television and films, Williams has had many successful roles in Broadway plays.

AT A GLANCE

Notable Films: *Brokeback Mountain* (2005), *Wendy and Lucy* (2008), *Blue Valentine* (2010), *Shutter Island* (2010), *My Week with Marilyn* (2011), *Take This Waltz* (2011), *Oz the Great and Powerful* (2013), *Manchester by the Sea* (2016), *All the Money in the World* (2017), *The Fabelmans* (2022)

Notable Awards: Golden Globe Awards, Best Actress—Motion Picture, Musical/Comedy (2012), Best Actress—Limited Series, Anthology Series, or Television Motion Picture (2020); New York Film Critics Circle Award, Best Supporting Actress (2016); Emmy Award, Outstanding Lead Actress in a Limited Series or Movie (2019); Screen Actors Guild Award, Outstanding Performance by a Female Actor in a Television Movie or Limited Series (2020)

After college, Robin Williams got his first jobs working in comedy clubs and then on television shows. In 1978, he landed his own television show, *Mork & Mindy*. This program was a showcase for his comedy talents. The success from the show launched him into movie roles.

HUMOR AND MORE

Williams's first major film role was as a disc jockey in *Good Morning, Vietnam*. It earned him an Academy Award nomination. He got a second nomination for his work in *Dead Poets Society*. In the popular movie *Mrs. Doubtfire*, Williams played a divorced dad who pretends to be a female nanny as a way to be close to his children. Although Williams took many

Robin Williams holds his Oscar during the 70th Academy Awards in 1998.

roles that highlighted his humor, he also played serious characters. In *The Fisher King*, Williams was a former professor. In *Good Will Hunting*, he played a psychiatrist. Williams won an Academy Award for *Good Will Hunting*.

It took more than four hours for Williams to get his makeup done to transform into Mrs. Doubtfire.

AT A GLANCE

Notable Films: *The World According to Garp* (1982), *Good Morning, Vietnam* (1987), *Dead Poets Society* (1989), *The Fisher King* (1991), *Aladdin* (1992), *Mrs. Doubtfire* (1993), *Good Will Hunting* (1997), *Patch Adams* (1998), *One Hour Photo* (2002), *Night at the Museum* (2006)

Notable Awards: Golden Globe Awards, Best Television Actor— Musical/Comedy (1979), Best Actor—Motion Picture, Musical/Comedy (1988, 1992, 1994), Special Achievement Award (1993), Cecil B. DeMille Award (2005); Grammy Awards, Best Comedy Recording (1980, 1988, 1989), Best Recording for Children (1989), Best Spoken Comedy Album (2003); Emmy Awards, Outstanding Individual Performance in a Variety or Music Program (1987, 1988); Academy Award, Best Supporting Actor (1998)

BRUCE WILLIS

Bruce Willis was born in 1955 at a US military base in West Germany. He studied acting in college. Then he moved to New York City. He got acting jobs in theaters and on television commercials. In the late 1980s, Willis gained attention for his performance as a detective in the television series *Moonlighting*. He also played a detective in the action film *Die Hard*. The movie was popular with audiences and brought Willis fame as an action hero.

Bruce Willis got a star on the Hollywood Walk of Fame in 2006.

WIDE-RANGING ROLES

Over the next two decades, Willis starred in many successful movies. The film genres were broad and included action, science fiction, and comedy.

Notable Films: *Die Hard* series (1988, 1990, 1995, 2007, 2013), *Pulp Fiction* (1994), *12 Monkeys* (1995), *The Fifth Element* (1997), *Armageddon* (1998), *The Sixth Sense* (1999), *Unbreakable* (2000), *Sin City* (2005), *Looper* (2012), *Moonrise Kingdom* (2012)

Notable Awards: Golden Globe Award, Best Television Actor—Musical/Comedy (1987); Emmy Awards, Outstanding Lead Actor in a Drama Series (1987), Outstanding Guest Actor in a Comedy Series (2000)

Willis often played characters who were sarcastic, funny, or tough. In the box-office hit *Pulp Fiction*, he played a boxer. In *Looper*, he played a hit man who travels through time.

In 2022, Willis's family announced that he would no longer be acting because he has dementia.

KATE WINSLET

Kate Winslet was a young adult when she appeared in *Heavenly Creatures*. A year later, in 1995, Winslet earned awards when she played the role of Marianne Dashwood in *Sense and Sensibility*. She also received her first Academy Award nomination for that role.

Kate Winslet was born in England and raised in the acting world. Her parents, grandparents, and uncle all had theater jobs.

Winslet became an international star after her performance in the widely popular movie *Titanic*. In that film, she played Rose DeWitt Bukater, a wealthy woman who feels trapped in her life and falls in love with a lower-class passenger. For her performance, Winslet received an Academy Award nomination for Best Actress.

ROLES TO REMEMBER

Winslet's acting success continued with the films *The Reader* and *Steve Jobs*. In *The Reader*, Winslet played a former guard at a World War II concentration camp. She received an Academy Award for her performance. In *Steve Jobs*, she played a marketing executive. In 2012, Queen Elizabeth II awarded Winslet with the prestigious Commander of the Most Excellent Order of the British Empire for her service to drama.

Kate Winslet worked with Leonardo DiCaprio in *Titanic*.

AT A GLANCE

Notable Films: *Heavenly Creatures* (1994), *Sense and Sensibility* (1995), *Jude* (1996), *Titanic* (1997), *Iris* (2001), *Eternal Sunshine of the Spotless Mind* (2004), *Little Children* (2006), *The Reader* (2008), *Revolutionary Road* (2008), *Steve Jobs* (2015)

Notable Awards: BAFTA Awards, Best Performance by an Actress in a Supporting Role (1996), Best Leading Actress (2009), Best Supporting Actress (2016); Academy Award, Best Actress (2009); Golden Globe Awards, Best Supporting Actress—Motion Picture (2009, 2016), Best Actress—Motion Picture, Drama (2009), Best Actress—Limited Series, Anthology Series, or Television Motion Picture (2022)

MICHELLE YEOH

Michelle Yeoh was born on August 6, 1962, in Malaysia. As a teenager, she trained in ballet. Her first acting roles were in Hong Kong films with lots of action and stunts.

Yeoh gained fame for playing a Chinese agent in *Tomorrow Never Dies*. In the movie *Crouching Tiger, Hidden Dragon*—a love story with plenty of action scenes—she played a warrior. The film was popular with audiences and won several Academy Awards.

Michelle Yeoh gained widespread fame for her role as a Chinese agent in *Tomorrow Never Dies*. This film is in the *James Bond* franchise.

EVERYTHING EVERYWHERE ALL AT ONCE

Yeoh had the lead role in the science-fiction comedy *Everything Everywhere All at Once*. It was a challenging role where she had

DID YOU KNOW?

Actors often use stuntpeople to perform dangerous scenes in movies. But Michelle Yeoh is famous for doing her own stunts. For instance, in the film *Police Story 3: Supercop*, she dropped from a bus onto a moving car and jumped a motorcycle onto a moving train.

AT A GLANCE

Notable Films: *Supercop* (1992), *Supercop 2* (1993), *Tomorrow Never Dies* (1997), *Crouching Tiger, Hidden Dragon* (2000), *Memoirs of a Geisha* (2005), *The Lady* (2011), *Guardians of the Galaxy Vol. 2* (2017), *Crazy Rich Asians* (2018), *Shang-Chi and the Legend of the Ten Rings* (2021), *Everything Everywhere All at Once* (2022)

Notable Awards: National Board of Review, Best Actress (2022); Golden Globe Award, Best Actress—Motion Picture, Musical/Comedy (2023); Screen Actors Guild Award, Female Actor in a Leading Role (2023); Academy Award, Best Actress (2023)

to play different versions of the same character. Yeoh won a Golden Globe Award and an Academy Award for Best Actress for her work in the movie. She was the first Asian woman to receive an Academy Award in that category.

Yeoh, *second from left*, stands with other Academy Award winners at the 2023 ceremony.

Zendaya's full name is Zendaya Maree Stoermer Coleman, but she works using just her first name. Her first acting roles were shows on the Disney Channel. Between 2010 and 2013, she starred in the Disney show *Shake It Up*, where she played a teenager striving to become a dancer.

FURTHERING HER ACTING SKILLS

Beyond the Disney Channel movies and shows, Zendaya's first film role was in *Spider-Man: Homecoming*. She also gained praise for her acting and singing in the musical *The Greatest Showman*. Zendaya received a Golden Globe Award and two Emmy Awards for her role in the HBO series *Euphoria*. In 2020, when she received the Emmy for Outstanding Lead Actress in a Drama Series, she was the youngest actor to win the award in that category. With the Emmy

In 2013, Zendaya released a musical album titled *Zendaya*. She also appeared on *Dancing with the Stars* that year. This is a reality television show where people compete in dancing.

In Zendaya's 2022 Emmy acceptance speech, she thanked everyone who made her role as Rue in *Euphoria* possible.

she received in 2022, Zendaya became the first Black woman to win that award twice. She has performed in two more *Spider-Man* movies, as well as the science-fiction movie *Dune*.

AT A GLANCE

Notable Films: *The Greatest Showman* (2017), *Spider-Man: Homecoming* (2017), *Smallfoot* (2018), *Spider-Man: Far From Home* (2019), *Spider-Man: No Way Home* (2021), *Space Jam: A New Legacy* (2021), *Malcolm & Marie* (2021), *Dune* (2021)

Notable Awards: Emmy Awards, Outstanding Lead Actress in a Drama Series (2020, 2022); Golden Globe Award, Best Performance by an Actress in a Television Series—Drama (2023)

GLOSSARY

archaeologist
A person who studies the material remains of past human life, such as pottery, jewelry, or monuments.

autism
A developmental disorder where people struggle with communication and social skills and often perform repetitive behaviors.

cabaret
A type of nightclub that provides entertainment.

counterculture
An alternative culture or lifestyle that conflicts with the established culture.

debut
A person's first appearance on the stage or on-screen.

discrimination
Unfair treatment of other people, usually because of race, age, or gender.

genocide
When a group of people are killed because of their nationality, ethnicity, race, or religion.

groupie
A fan who follows a famous person or group trying to meet or get to know the person or people.

gunslinger
A person who shoots a gun well, usually in a Western film.

martial arts
Combat sports and self-defense skills, such as judo, karate, or kung fu.

segregation
To separate groups of people based on race, gender, ethnicity, or other factors.

sequel
In films, a movie that continues the story of an earlier movie.

stand-up comedy
Shows where a comedian tells jokes to the audience from a stage.

trilogy
Three related films, plays, or novels.

valedictorian
A graduating student who has the best rank in his or her class.

TO LEARN MORE

FURTHER READINGS

Kelly, Christa. *The Superhero Encyclopedia*. Abdo, 2024.

Murray, Laura K. *The Movie Encyclopedia*. Abdo, 2024.

Yacka, Douglas. *Where Is Broadway?* Penguin Workshop, 2019.

ONLINE RESOURCES

To learn more about actors, please visit **abdobooklinks.com** or scan this QR code. These links are routinely monitored and updated to provide the most current information available.

INDEX

PHOTO CREDITS

ABDOBOOKS.COM

Published by Abdo Reference, a division of ABDO, PO Box 398166, Minneapolis, Minnesota 55439. Copyright © 2024 by Abdo Consulting Group, Inc. International copyrights reserved in all countries. No part of this book may be reproduced in any form without written permission from the publisher. Encyclopedias™ is a trademark and logo of Abdo Reference.

102023
012024

THIS BOOK CONTAINS
RECYCLED MATERIALS

Editor: Alyssa Sorenson
Series Designer: Colleen McLaren
Production Designers: Joshua Olson and Ryan Gale

LIBRARY OF CONGRESS CONTROL NUMBER: 2023939617

PUBLISHER'S CATALOGING-IN-PUBLICATION DATA

Names: McKinney, Donna B., author.
Title: The actor encyclopedia / by Donna B. McKinney
Description: Minneapolis, Minnesota: Abdo Reference, 2024 | Series: Entertainment encyclopedias | Includes online resources and index.
Identifiers: ISBN 9781098292980 (lib. bdg.) | ISBN 9798384910923 (ebook)
Subjects: LCSH: Actors--Juvenile literature. | Actresses--Juvenile literature. | Acting--Juvenile literature. | Entertainers--Juvenile literature. | Acting--History--Juvenile literature. | Encyclopedias and dictionaries --Juvenile literature.
Classification: DDC 790.2--dc23